MW01062756

"Studies of Paul's three Pastoral Lette
dress. Claire Smith rightly centers on the God
people for himself. This places the emphasis where the text does and advances
the teachings and admonitions that surely renewed faith, direction, and hope
in Timothy, in Titus, and in their congregations. Smith's exceptionally clear
and flowing exposition of the letters to Timothy and Titus offers the same
refreshing benefit to readers, the church, and the world today."

Robert W. Yarbrough, Professor of New Testament, Covenant
Theological Seminary

"With sound scholarship and insightful clarity, Claire Smith zooms out from
the text of these three epistles, helping readers to see the overriding themes
and ideas Paul communicates, and enabling readers to trace his arguments,
understand his terms, and grasp his message."

Nancy Guthrie, author and Bible teacher

"This is an excellent guide to three New Testament epistles that are vitally
important for the life of the church. Smith structures her introduction around
their major themes: the sovereign purposes of God, the need for and nature of
salvation, and the proclamation of the message and its outworking in the life
of the Christian community. A great place to begin to understand what God
is saying to his pilgrim people here on earth, as we await the final outworking
of his plan for us and the whole of creation."

Gerald Bray, Research Professor of Divinity, Beeson Divinity School;
Director of Research, Latimer Trust

"This accessible volume provides a very useful sketch of the theology of each
of Paul's letters to Timothy and Titus. Readers will find in Claire Smith a
competent and reliable guide for studying these eminently relevant missives
to Paul's apostolic delegates."

Andreas J. Köstenberger, Theologian in Residence, Fellowship Raleigh,
North Carolina; Research Professor of Biblical Studies, Palm Beach
Atlantic University

"*The Appearing of God Our Savior* is classic Claire Smith. It is clear and compel-
ling and will help you be a better reader of God's word. Smith shows us that
life is always about how God orders things. Therefore, every part of our lives
is to conform to God's purposes and plans. We may suffer now as we live this
way, but we are blessed and saved for eternity through Christ Jesus."

Jane Tooher, Faculty, Moore Theological College, Sydney

"Here is a masterful demonstration that the letters to Timothy and Titus contain much more than ecclesiological tidbits. Pastors and other Bible teachers will find in this volume a lucid summation of God's redemptive arrangement: the one God who desires to save a people for himself, the one mediator—Jesus Christ—who accomplishes the salvation of God's people, the Spirit who indwells and empowers, and the human agents through whom God's saving word advances. This will remain one of my go-to theological resources as I preach and teach the letters to Paul's delegates."

Dillon T. Thornton, Lead Pastor, Faith Community Church, Seminole, Florida

"Claire Smith has gifted us with a remarkable resource that delves into the theological and pastoral depths of Paul's letters to Timothy and Titus. Often these letters are viewed only through the lens of specific debates. However, Smith skillfully encourages us to take a broader perspective, highlighting how the letters convey profound truths about the God who saves us from sin and death through his Son, Jesus Christ. Smith connects these truths to the practical realities of human relationships, church life, and pastoral ministry. While clearly the result of her thorough exegetical analysis and scholarly expertise, the book remains clear, accessible, and highly engaging."

Lionel Windsor, Lecturer in New Testament, Moore Theological College, Sydney

"The New Testament letters to Timothy and Titus address a number of critically important issues in the life of the churches in Ephesus and Crete at the time of writing. Claire Smith's helpful study carefully explores the big ideas about God and his purposes that shape the apostle Paul's understanding of and response to these issues. Those of us who tend to focus on the details of the particular texts will be helped to see how the appearing of God our Savior is the wonderful reality that, in different ways, illuminates each of these letters. Bible students and teachers will benefit from this perceptive bird's-eye view."

John Woodhouse, Former Principal, Moore Theological College, Sydney

"The Pastoral Epistles are essential for the health of the church of Christ. They are core study material for all church leaders and Christian workers. Churches benefit from every member being familiar with them. This concise study identifies and examines the key theological themes in each letter and thus provides an outstanding resource for any wishing to understand and teach this vital material. I found myself profoundly encouraged by Claire Smith's work."

William Taylor, Rector, St Helen's Bishopsgate, London

"This excellent book fills a long-standing need for a thorough assessment of the theology expressed in these letters without the undue but widespread skepticism about the letters. With clear and accessible writing, Smith beautifully articulates the theology of the Pastoral Epistles, showing also how it fits with the rest of Pauline, and indeed New Testament, theology, making this a wonderful resource for anyone studying 1–2 Timothy and Titus."

Ray Van Neste, Dean of the School of Theology and Missions and Vice President for University Ministries, Union University

"Claire Smith expertly expounds 1–2 Timothy and Titus in this excellent entry to the New Testament Theology series. These apostolic letters not only engage pressing challenges of the early church but also instruct the church in every age to marvel at the saving plan of God, to hold fast to God-breathed Scriptures, to endure suffering, and to love Christ's appearing. Highly recommended!"

Brian J. Tabb, President and Professor of Biblical Studies, Bethlehem College and Seminary

"Claire Smith's study of these epistles helps us to elevate our gaze to the majestic narrative of God's redemptive plan in Christ. Her exploration of the themes reveals that the heart of these Pastoral Letters lies not in household and church rules but in a revelation of God's character and his mission in the world to save sinners and transform a people for himself. Smith's work will help Christian leaders and all God's people to stand courageously firm in God's revealed truth and live gospel-shaped lives while we await the glorious appearing of Jesus."

Carmelina Read, Dean of Women, Christ College, Presbyterian Theological College

The Appearing of God Our Savior

New Testament Theology

Edited by Thomas R. Schreiner and Brian S. Rosner

The Appearing of God Our Savior

A Theology of 1 and 2 Timothy and Titus

Claire S. Smith

WHEATON, ILLINOIS

Cover design: Kevin Lipp

First printing 2025

Printed in the United States of America

Word counts of Greek words from the New Testament have been obtained from Accordance 12.3.6 © Oaktree Software, Inc. August 2019.

Trade paperback ISBN: 978-1-4335-7652-2
ePub ISBN: 978-1-4335-7655-3
PDF ISBN: 978-1-4335-7653-9

Library of Congress Cataloging-in-Publication Data

Names: Smith, Claire S. (Claire Seymour), 1960– author.
Title: The appearing of God our savior : a Theology of 1 and 2 Timothy and Titus / Claire S. Smith.
Description: Wheaton, Illinois : Crossway, 2025. | Series: New Testament theology | Includes bibliographical references and index.
Identifiers: LCCN 2024010286 (print) | LCCN 2024010287 (ebook) | ISBN 9781433576522 (trade paperback) | ISBN 9781433576539 (pdf) | ISBN 9781433576553 (epub)
Subjects: LCSH: Bible. Timothy. | Bible. Titus. | Jesus Christ.
Classification: LCC BS2745.3 .S74 2025 (print) | LCC BS2745.3 (ebook) | DDC 227/.8306—dc23/eng/20240523
LC record available at https://lccn.loc.gov/2024010286
LC ebook record available at https://lccn.loc.gov/2024010287

Crossway is a publishing ministry of Good News Publishers.

VP		34	33	32	31	30	29	28	27	26	25
15	14	13	12	11	10	9	8	7	6	5	4	3	2	1

For my sister Barbara
For her exemplary care of our mother
1 Timothy 5:4, 16

Contents

Series Preface

THERE ARE REMARKABLY FEW TREATMENTS of the big ideas of single books of the New Testament. Readers can find brief coverage in Bible dictionaries, in some commentaries, and in New Testament theologies, but such books are filled with other information and are not devoted to unpacking the theology of each New Testament book in its own right. Technical works concentrating on various themes of New Testament theology often have a narrow focus, treating some aspect of the teaching of, say, Matthew or Hebrews in isolation from the rest of the book's theology.

The New Testament Theology series seeks to fill this gap by providing students of Scripture with readable book-length treatments of the distinctive teaching of each New Testament book or collection of books. The volumes approach the text from the perspective of biblical theology. They pay due attention to the historical and literary dimensions of the text, but their main focus is on presenting the teaching of particular New Testament books about God and his relations to the world on their own terms, maintaining sight of the Bible's overarching narrative and Christocentric focus. Such biblical theology is of fundamental importance to biblical and expository preaching and informs exegesis, systematic theology, and Christian ethics.

The twenty volumes in the series supply comprehensive, scholarly, and accessible treatments of theological themes from an evangelical perspective. We envision them being of value to students, preachers, and interested laypeople. When preparing an expository sermon series, for example, pastors can find a healthy supply of informative commentaries, but there are few options for coming to terms with the overall teaching of each book of the New Testament. As well as being useful in sermon and Bible study preparation, the volumes will also be of value as textbooks in college and seminary exegesis classes. Our prayer is that they contribute to a deeper understanding of and commitment to the kingdom and glory of God in Christ.

The authenticity of the Pastoral Epistles is often questioned, but even when they are accepted as authentic, they are too often assigned a subsidiary status in Paul's thought. Claire Smith demonstrates in her insightful treatment that these letters proclaim the gospel, the good news that God in Jesus Christ is our Savior and Lord. At the same time, God's saving work touches earth, reaching out to human beings and forming a new community—the church. We see, then, that God's saving work brings order and structure and truth to God's people. Such order and structure doesn't quench life but causes God's people to blossom and flourish. God's saving work has a transformative impact on the lives of those who are redeemed so that God's people display God's character and grace to the world.

Thomas R. Schreiner and Brian S. Rosner

Preface

AS PEOPLE WHO SPEND OUR LIVES studying and teaching God's word, we can easily pigeonhole books in the Bible. We turn to Romans for teaching on justification by faith; 1 Corinthians for our corporate life as the body of Christ; Philippians for church unity; and, when it comes to the focus of this current book, 1 Timothy for gender relations and the role of women in the church; 2 Timothy for ministry training; and perhaps Titus for church order or mentoring among women. There's nothing necessarily wrong with that. But it can mean our pigeonholing takes us straight into the nitty-gritty of specific texts before we've done the Google Earth view and considered the book as a whole.

That's certainly been my experience with this project. The letters are familiar. I've studied them closely over the years. But it has been reorienting (and rewarding) to step back and explore the main themes and to see that, despite the intensely practical nature of the letters, they say more about *God and his project to save a people for himself* than they do about us. I hope your eyes and hearts are similarly lifted to God our Savior!

I am very grateful to Drs. Tom Schreiner and Brian Rosner for the invitation to contribute to this series, and for their warm fellowship and encouragement along the way. There are others to thank, too. Anyone working on Paul's letters to Timothy and Titus owes a debt of thanks to Dr. Chuck Bumgardner, who curates the website pastoralepistles .com and is himself an invaluable resource on these letters. I was also greatly helped by the feedback of friends and fellow researchers, Talar

Khatchoyan, Archdeacon Kara Hartley, and Drs. Lionel Windsor, John Percival, and Rob Smith, who gave their precious time and wisdom to read the manuscript as it neared the finish line. I'm grateful to my women's Bible study groups at our previous and current churches, for their faithful prayers and pastoral care. As always, I am thankful for my husband, Rob, my greatest encourager. Thanks, too, go to editor Thom Notaro and the rest of the team at Crossway for bringing this book to publication. My deepest thanks go to God—for saving this foremost of sinners, and for the goodness and sufficiency of his word and the incredible blessing of being its student and sharing it with others. "To [him] be honor and glory forever and ever" (1 Tim. 1:17).

Claire S. Smith
December 2023

Abbreviations

AB	Anchor Bible
AT	Author's translation
BBR	*Bulletin for Biblical Research*
BBRSup	*Bulletin for Biblical Research, Supplements*
BDAG	Danker, Frederick W., Walter Bauer, William F. Arndt, and F. Wilbur Gingrich. *Greek-English Lexicon of the New Testament and Other Early Christian Literature*. 3rd ed. Chicago: University of Chicago Press, 2000
BST	Bible Speaks Today
BTCP	Biblical Theology for Christian Proclamation
BTINT	*Biblical Theological Introduction to the New Testament: The Gospel Realized*. Edited by Michael J. Kruger. Wheaton, IL: Crossway, 2016
CBC	Cornerstone Biblical Commentary
CNTUOT	*Commentary on the New Testament Use of the Old Testament*. Edited by G. K. Beale and D. A. Carson. Grand Rapids: Baker Academic, 2007
DJG	Dictionary of Jesus and the Gospels. Edited by Joel B. Green, Jeannine K. Brown, and Nicholas Perrin. 2nd ed. Downers Grove, IL: InterVarsity Press, 2013 (ProQuest Ebook Central, https://ebookcentral.proquest.com/lib /moore/detail.action?docID=3316699)

DPL	*Dictionary of Paul and His Letters.* Edited by Gerald F. Hawthorne, Ralph P. Martin, and Daniel G. Reid. Downers Grove, IL: InterVarsity Press, 1993
ECC	Eerdmans Critical Commentary
EvQ	*Evangelical Quarterly*
EWTG	*Entrusted with the Gospel: Paul's Theology in the Pastoral Epistles.* Edited by Andreas J. Köstenberger and Terry L. Wilder. Nashville: B&H Academic, 2010
HBT	*Horizons in Biblical Theology*
IBS	*Irish Biblical Studies*
ICC	International Critical Commentary
Int	*Interpretation*
ITC	International Theological Commentary
JETS	*Journal of the Evangelical Theological Society*
JSNTSup	Journal for the Study of the New Testament Supplement Series
JSPL	*Journal for the Study of Paul and His Letters*
LSJ	Liddell, Henry George, Robert Scott, and Henry Stuart Jones. *Greek-English Lexicon.* 9th ed. with revised supplement. Oxford: Clarendon, 1996
LXX	Septuagint
NAC	New American Commentary
NDBT	*New Dictionary of Biblical Theology.* Edited by T. Desmond Alexander and Brian S. Rosner. Leicester, UK: Inter-Varsity Press, 2000
NIBC	New International Biblical Commentary
NICNT	New International Commentary on the New Testament
NIDNTT	*New International Dictionary of New Testament Theology.* Edited by Colin Brown. 4 vols. Grand Rapids, MI: Zondervan, 1975–1978
NIGTC	New International Greek Testament Commentary
NTS	*New Testament Studies*
PBM	Paternoster Biblical Monographs

PE	Pastoral Epistles
PNTC	The Pillar New Testament Commentary
REGW	*"Ready for Every Good Work" (Titus 3:1): Implicit Ethics in the Letter to Titus.* Edited by Ruben Zimmermann and Dogara Ishaya Manomi. Contexts and Norms of New Testament Ethics 13. Wissenschaftliche Untersuchungen zum Neuen Testament 484. Tübingen: Mohr Siebeck, 2022
SNTSU	*Studien zum Neuen Testament und seiner Umwelt*
ST	*Studia Theologica*
STR	*Southeastern Theological Review*
TENTS	Texts and Editions for New Testament Study
THNTC	Two Horizons New Testament Commentary
TNTC	Tyndale New Testament Commentaries
WBC	Word Biblical Commentary
WTJ	*Westminster Theological Journal*
WUNT	Wissenschaftliche Untersuchungen zum Neuen Testament
ZNW	*Zeitschrift für die neutestamentliche Wissenschaft und die Kunde der älteren Kirche*

Bible Versions Cited

www.zondervan.com. The "NIV" and "New International Version" are trademarks registered in the United States Patent and Trademark Office by Biblica, Inc.™

Scripture quotations marked NKJV are taken from the New King James Version®. Copyright © 1982 by Thomas Nelson. Used by permission. All rights reserved.

Scripture quotations marked RSV are from the Revised Standard Version of the Bible, copyright © 1946, 1952, and 1971 by the Division of Christian Education of the National Council of the Churches of Christ in the United States of America. Used by permission. All rights reserved.

Scripture quotations marked YLT are taken from Young's Literal Translation, 1898. Public domain.

Introduction

Who, What, When, and Why?

THE LETTERS TO TIMOTHY AND TITUS[1] divide readers perhaps more than any other books in the New Testament. They're embraced as the last canonical words of the beloved apostle Paul or maligned as fictitious works of forgery. They are the go-to guide for authentic gospel ministry or mark the church's departure from the apostolic era into arid formalism and hierarchical institutionalism. They present the beauty of God-ordained complementary gender relations or are guilty of misogynistic patriarchalism.

Some interpreters decry the letters' theological poverty and think them unworthy of Paul. Others see them comfortably aligned with Paul's teaching and treasure their theological gems, for instance, about Christ's coming into the world "to save sinners" (1 Tim. 1:15), the God-breathed nature of Scripture (2 Tim. 3:16), the unstoppable gospel (2 Tim. 2:9), the future appearing of "our great God and Savior Jesus Christ" (Titus 2:13), and "fighting the good fight" of faith (1 Tim. 6:12; 2 Tim. 4:7).

There are many reasons for these conflicting reactions, but behind almost all of them is the question of authorship.

Authorship of the Letters

The opening verses of all three letters unambiguously claim that they are from the apostle Paul (1 Tim. 1:1; 2 Tim. 1:1; Titus 1:1). Until the

---

1   Explanation of this preferred collective term is found below.

early nineteenth century this claim stood largely unchallenged, but since then it's been broadly rejected by critical interpreters. This has meant that issues of authorship have dominated the study of the letters among *both* those who deny Pauline authorship *and* those who accept it.[2] Authorship has become the lens through which every aspect of the letters is viewed, including their theology.

Interpreters who reject Pauline authorship claim the letters were written after Paul's death by those seeking to sound like the apostle either to preserve his legacy and apply his teaching to new situations or (more self-interestedly) to assume Paul's identity and authority to advance their own agenda. Either way, the letters are viewed as pseudonymous, and the author and recipients and their situations are literary constructs, not real. It's not Paul's voice or theology we hear but Pauline "tradition" or, at best, fragments of the "real Paul" pasted into someone else's work, skeptics argue.[3]

Typically, their objections have concentrated on five features (vocabulary, style, false teaching opposed, ecclesiology, and theology), where the letters to Timothy and Titus are seen to differ from Paul's so-called "undisputed" letters. However, the nature and significance of these differences have been overstated and are increasingly seen as misplaced in the first place.[4] The evidence weighs against a pseudonymous author and a post-apostolic date.[5]

2   For a recent survey of the issues, see Jermo van Nes, "The Pastoral Epistles: Common Themes, Individual Compositions? An Introduction to the Quest for the Origin(s) of the Letters to Timothy and Titus," *JSPL* 9 (2019): 6–29. See, also, introductions to most commentaries, in particular: Luke Timothy Johnson, *The First and Second Letters to Timothy*, AB 35A (New York: Doubleday, 2001), 20–97; Philip H. Towner, *The Letters to Timothy and Titus*, NICNT (Grand Rapids, MI: Eerdmans, 2006), 27–53; Andreas J. Köstenberger, *Commentary on 1–2 Timothy and Titus*, BTCP (Nashville: Holman Reference, 2017), 1–54; Robert W. Yarbrough, *The Letters to Timothy and Titus*, PNTC (Grand Rapids, MI: Eerdmans, 2018), 69–90.

3   For a critique of such views, see Terry L. Wilder, "Pseudonymity, the New Testament, and the Pastoral Epistles," in *EWTG* 28–51.

4   See Stanley E. Porter, "The Pastoral Epistles: Common Themes, Individual Compositions. Concluding Reflections," *JSPL* 9 (2019): 167–74.

5   See Eckhard J. Schnabel, "Paul, Timothy, and Titus: The Assumption of a Pseudonymous Author and of Pseudonymous Recipients in the Light of Literary, Theological, and Histori-

There have always been those who have accepted the prima facie claim of the ascriptions and the testimony of the early church that all three letters were written by Paul.[6] More recently, too, the tide has begun to turn, and interpreters across the theological divide are affirming Pauline authorship.[7] Some among that number see the input of a scribe as the reason for differences with Paul's other letters (cf. Rom. 16:22),[8] although the absence of a scribe or of co-senders might equally explain these differences. My view is that Paul is the author of each of the three letters, without significant input from a scribe, if any.

We don't know exactly when the letters were written, and there are difficulties fitting them into the chronology of Acts and Paul's other letters. But this doesn't preclude Pauline authorship.[9] Most likely, Paul was released from the imprisonment recorded in Acts 28, had a subsequent ministry during which 1 Timothy and Titus were written (ca. AD 62–65), then was imprisoned again and died in Rome (ca. AD 65–67).[10] Second Timothy is his last letter, written during that final imprisonment.

I have one further observation about their authorship. Liberal scholar A. T. Hanson wrote that anyone writing about the letters to Timothy and Titus "must begin by stating whether he believes they are Pauline or not, and if not, in what circumstances he believes they were written."[11] That's because views on authorship and the related matters of dating and historical context play a significant role in an interpreter's hermeneutical

cal Evidence," in *Do Historical Matters Matter to Faith? A Critical Appraisal of Modern and Postmodern Approaches to Scripture*, ed. James K. Hoffmeier and Dennis R. Magary (Wheaton, IL: Crossway, 2012), 383–403.

6   Cf. Muratorian Fragment, lines 59–63 (ca. AD 180–200); Irenaeus, *Against Heresies* 3.3.3 (ca. AD 175). For history of reception and interpretation, see Gerald L. Bray, *The Pastoral Epistles*, ITC (London: T&T Clark, 2019), 51–68.

7   See Yarbrough, *Letters*, 72–78; Johnson, *Letters*, 92–94, 98–99.

8   So, for example, William D. Mounce, *Pastoral Epistles*, WBC 46 (Nashville: Thomas Nelson, 2000), cxxvii–cxxix; George W. Knight, *Commentary on the Pastoral Epistles*, NIGTC (Grand Rapids, MI: Eerdmans, 1992), 48–52.

9   Johnson, *Letters*, 61–62.

10   Köstenberger, *Timothy and Titus*, 24–32.

11   Anthony T. Hanson, "The Use of the Old Testament in the Pastoral Epistles," *IBS* 3 (1981): 203.

approach and conclusions about the letters. Views on authorship affect
the whole enterprise. This means that as students of these letters who
receive them as divinely inspired, truth-telling Scripture, we need to
read scholarly resources with the interpreter's views on authorship front
of mind, even if they come from well-loved, accomplished scholars.[12]

The "Pastoral Epistles" Label

The three works have been known as the Pastoral Epistles since at least
the early eighteenth century[13] and, from the time of the early church,
have been recognized as forming a group within the New Testament
Epistles addressing the ordering and exercise of ministry, and the
instruction and discipline of church members.[14]

There is a certain logic to the grouping and adjective "pastoral." There
is no denying that the letters have distinctive shared characteristics.
They are the only letters in the New Testament primarily addressed
to Paul's coworkers.[15] They were written late in the apostle's life. They
have distinctive vocabulary.[16] Much of what they address relates to
church ministry.[17] They deal with opponents who have arisen from
within the churches and are within reach of pastoral discipline. And
they're a substitute for Paul's physical presence, so that, whether his

12 For example, I. Howard Marshall proposes a process of "allonymity," where, after Paul's
death, a follower of Paul composed the letters using authentic notes or fragments from
him. Marshall believes the theology of the letters shares the "same coherent core" with
Paul's but also differs from it: e.g., "The Christology of the PE goes beyond that of the
genuine Pauline epistles in various ways." *The Pastoral Epistles*, ICC (Edinburgh: T&T
Clark, 1999), 83–108 (quoting p. 101).

13 Donald Guthrie, *The Pastoral Epistles*, TNTC (1957; repr., Leicester: Inter-Varsity Press,
1984), 11.

14 Since at least the Muratorian Fragment.

15 However, church members are also in view in the plural greetings (1 Tim. 6:21; 2 Tim.
4:22; Titus 3:15).

16 E.g., *eusebeia* (godliness); *hygiainousa didaskalia* (sound doctrine); *epignōsis alētheias*
(knowledge of the truth); and distinctive use of words: *sōtēr* (Savior); *epiphaneia* (appearing); *pistos ho logos* (trustworthy saying).

17 E.g., church discipline (1 Tim. 1:18–20; 2 Tim. 2:24–26; Titus 1:13–16), ordering the
church (1 Tim. 3:1–13, 15; 5:17–22; 2 Tim. 2:2; Titus 1:5–9), false teaching (1 Tim. 1:4;
2 Tim. 4:4; Titus 1:14).

absence is through distance or death (1 Tim. 3:15; 2 Tim. 1:4; 4:9, 21; Titus 1:5; 3:12), Timothy and Titus, and those after them, will have apostolic instruction about how the gospel of God's salvation in Christ is to be faithfully preserved, defended, advanced, and proclaimed until Christ Jesus appears in glory. It's no surprise, then, that they have been recognized as a subgroup within the Pauline corpus.

But even at a surface level, there are real differences. They have different recipients, Timothy and Titus, and churches in two locations, with different cultures and status within the Roman Empire: Ephesus, a significant city in Asia Minor (1 Tim. 1:3; 2 Tim. 1:18; 4:12; 2:17 with 1 Tim. 1:20), and Crete, a large island in the Mediterranean Sea (Titus 1:5).[18]

There are similarities *and* differences in the social and theological challenges facing the churches.[19] The false teaching in both locations had Jewish elements and involved speculation, genealogies, myths (1 Tim. 1:3–7; 4:7; 2 Tim. 4:4; Titus 1:10–16; 3:9), and ascetic concerns for ritual purity (1 Tim. 4:3; Titus 1:15). The opponents were immoral and greedy (1 Tim. 1:19; 4:2; 6:5–10; 2 Tim. 3:1–6; Titus 1:11, 15–16; 3:11). But the false claims about resurrection plaguing the Ephesian church (2 Tim. 2:18; cf. 1 Tim. 4:1–3)[20] don't feature in Titus; and the churches (1 Tim. 3:6; 5:17–20; Titus 1:5) and influence of the opponents appear less established in Crete than Ephesus (1 Tim. 1:18–20; 2 Tim. 2:17; 4:14; Titus 1:10–11; 3:10).

The delegates themselves had different cultural origins and different contact points with Paul's mission. Timothy's mother and grandmother were Jewish (2 Tim. 1:5; 3:14), but his father was Greek (Acts 16:1, 3). Titus was a full Gentile convert (Gal. 2:3). Both had accompanied Paul and been deputized for him and knew him and his theology (Timothy: 1 Tim. 1:3; cf. Acts 17:14; 19:22; 1 Cor. 4:17; 16:10–11; Phil. 2:19;

---

18 See S. M. Baugh, "A Foreign World: Ephesus in the First Century," in *Women in the Church: An Interpretation and Application of 1 Timothy 2:9–15*, 3rd ed., ed. Andreas J. Köstenberger and Thomas R. Schreiner (Wheaton, IL: Crossway, 2016), 25–64; George M. Wieland, "Roman Crete and the Letter to Titus," *NTS* 55 (2009): 338–54; Yarbrough, *Letters*, 46–51.

19 See Towner, *Letters*, 41–53.

20 Towner, *Letters*, 295n45.

1 Thess. 3:2; Titus: 2 Cor. 7:6–7; 12:18; Gal. 2:1; 2 Tim. 4:10). Each was Paul's "child" (*teknon*) in the faith, although the bond appears to have been closer with Timothy ("beloved," 2 Tim. 1:2).

The letters were also written at different points in Paul's life, and different stages in the life of the churches in Ephesus and Crete. We know that Paul had a long and fruitful ministry in Ephesus and a significant history with church leaders there (Acts 19; 20:17–38), but there's no similar record of his ministry on Crete (Acts 27:7–13; cf. 2:11). He may have ministered there, but Titus's anticipated role is not dependent upon it (Titus 1:5).

The title "Pastoral Epistles" can obscure these differences, but it can also facilitate a corpus reading that harmonizes the messages and theology of the letters and isolates them from Paul's other epistles. The "pastoral" adjective itself can direct attention away from other key aspects of the letters. With other interpreters, then, I prefer the title "the letters to Timothy and Titus," as this groups the letters without obscuring their individuality or prejudging their content.[21]

How to Use This Book

In keeping with this, and unlike many resources on the three letters, I have studied each one on its own. The upside of this is that the distinctive theology of each can be appreciated, even as we recognize the coherent theology of the same apostolic author. The downside is that to avoid repetition I've not always restated in detail what I have said earlier. For instance, Paul uses "Savior" (*sōtēr*) differently in each letter, but the Old Testament, Jewish, and Greco-Roman background to the title remains the same, and so I have not repeated it in full. Also, at points, I've contrasted an aspect of one letter with the other two. That is, while the three parts of this book correspond to the three letters, not everything said about each letter is in its designated part! My recommendation, therefore, is to read the whole book, so nothing is missed.

---

21 For recognition of differences, see Yarbrough, *Letters*, 11–40; Towner, *Letters*, 27–89; Köstenberger and Wilder, *EWTG* 52–83, 105–72, 241–67; Bray, *Pastoral Epistles*, 38–43.

PART 1

---

1 TIMOTHY

The Only God

1

The God Who Saves

AT FIRST GLANCE, 1 TIMOTHY IS CONCERNED with pressing local issues. Paul instructs Timothy to stay in Ephesus to silence those leading God's people away from the truth by teaching "different doctrine" (1:3; 6:3), and to ensure that believers behave properly as members of God's household (3:15). He tells Timothy that his own life, faith, beliefs, and teaching are to be blameless and exemplary, unlike the "fierce wolves" about whom Paul had prophetically warned the Ephesian elders (Acts 20:29–30). The letter also functions to equip and (re-)authorize Timothy as Paul's delegate (1 Tim. 1:3, 18; 6:13–14, 20; cf. 3:14–15), and to do so before the whole church, including its leadership (6:21).

However, closer consideration shows that 1 Timothy is primarily about God.[1] This is not just a confessional claim about all Scripture. In terms of the words used in the letter, "God" (*theos*) occurs more than any other noun (twenty-two times);[2] Christ Jesus is mentioned fifteen times; and the Spirit, twice (3:16; 4:1). And the primacy of God is more than statistics. The main theme of the letter is God's desire to save a people for himself. The gospel is his (1:11). The plan of salvation is his

1   Robert W. Yarbrough, *The Letters to Timothy and Titus*, PNTC (Grand Rapids, MI: Eerdmans, 2018), 13–14.
2   Yarbrough, *Letters*, 13. *Theos*, twenty-two times: 1:1, 2, 4, 11, 17; 2:3, 5 (2x); 3:5, 15 (2x); 4:3, 4, 5, 10; 5:4, 5, 21; 6:1, 11, 13, 17; cf. 6:16. Christ Jesus, twelve times: 1:1 (2x), 2, 12, 14, 15, 16; 2:5; 3:13; 4:6; 5:21; 6:13. Jesus Christ, two times: 6:3, 14. Christ: 5:11.

(2:4–7). The church is his household. Paul and Timothy are doing his work (1:18; 2:7; 4:6).

In short, who God is and how he is toward those he saves are integral to the message of the letter. Our study then begins by exploring what 1 Timothy says about the triune God who saves.

The Blessed God of the Gospel

Paul uses several designations for God in this letter: God is Savior, Father, the living God, the only God, King of kings, Lord of lords, and more. Paul also describes God: he is blessed, immortal, and invisible, he dwells in unapproachable light, and more. These divine titles and descriptions provide a framework for exploring the presentation of God in the letter, and, as we shall see, they are vital to its message. Some have rich backgrounds in the Old Testament in connection with God's self-revelation and acts in salvation history. Some identify his relationship to creation and humanity. And some speak to his uniqueness and supremacy against rival claimants to divinity and devotion.

The effect of these many titles and descriptions is to stress that the *same* God, who rules all things and who previously acted on Israel's behalf, now *in Christ Jesus* has accomplished his eschatological salvation plan for *all peoples*, Jew and Gentile, and that there is no other way to be saved.

God Our Savior

"Savior" is the first and the most frequent title for God in 1 Timothy (*sōtēr*, 1:1; 2:3; 4:10). At one level, this is not surprising. The consistent message of Scripture is that God is a God who saves. The Greek translation of the Old Testament (LXX) applies this title almost exclusively to God.[3] God himself declares that he is the *only* Savior, and there is no other (Isa. 45:21–22).

His deliverance of his people, Israel, from slavery in Egypt serves as a paradigm for his saving interventions (Ex. 20:2–3; Deut. 6:20–23; cf.

---

3 See George Wieland, *The Significance of Salvation: A Study of Salvation Language in the Pastoral Epistles*, PBM (Milton Keynes, UK: Paternoster, 2006), 21–27.

Isa. 43:14–21), and his saving deeds are an expression of his kingship over them (1 Chron. 16:23–36; Ps. 98; cf. Luke 1:47, 52) and define his relationship with them (e.g., *my/your* Savior," 1 Sam. 10:19 LXX; Ps. 25:5 [24:5 LXX]; Isa. 12:2 LXX).[4] Yet the Old Testament prophets looked forward to a final, future salvation that would be accomplished by God's messianic King/Son and would involve *all* nations (Isa. 11:1–10; 52:10; Zech. 9:9–10). The message of the New Testament is that God has now done this in the incarnate life, death, resurrection, and ascension of his Son, Jesus Christ (e.g., Rom. 5:6–10; 1 Cor. 15:3–6; 1 Pet. 1:10–12).

Given all this, we might expect to find the title "Savior" frequently in the New Testament. But we don't! It appears just twenty-four times,[5] ten of those in the letters to Timothy and Titus: for God the Father in 1 Timothy and Titus (1 Tim. 1:1; 2:3; 4:10; Titus 1:3; 2:10; 3:4); and for Christ Jesus in 2 Timothy and Titus (2 Tim. 1:10; Titus 1:4; 2:13; 3:6). It is one of a handful of terms whose frequency is distinctive to these three letters. It is possible that Paul uses the title in these letters for polemical effect, given the use of "savior" language for Greek gods and/or the ruler-cult, where Roman emperors were worshiped as divine saviors and benefactors.[6]

But the title is best understood in continuity (and discontinuity) with its Old Testament background. The Savior God of 1 Timothy *is* the Savior God of the Old Testament, but rather than having an exclusive relationship with one nation, he has now provided salvation for *all* who believe (2:4–6; 4:10): both Jew and Gentile (2:7; cf. Rom. 3:29–30; Gal. 3:28; Col. 3:11). The logic goes like this: now, as then, there is only

4 Andreas J. Köstenberger, *Commentary on 1–2 Timothy and Titus*, BTCP (Nashville: Holman Reference, 2017), 433n248. Cf. Intertestamental literature: Judith 9:11; Wis. 16:7; Sir. 51:1; Bar. 4:22; 1 Macc. 4:30; 3 Macc. 6:29, 32; 7:16.

5 Luke 1:47; 2:11; John 4:42; Acts 5:31; 13:23; Eph. 5:23; Phil. 3:20; 2 Pet. 1:1, 11; 2:20; 3:2, 18; 1 John 4:14; Jude 25.

6 See Ben Witherington III, *A Socio-Rhetorical Commentary on Titus, 1–2 Timothy and 1–3 John*, vol. 1 of *Letters and Homilies for Hellenized Christians* (Downers Grove, IL: InterVarsity, 2006), ProQuest Ebook Central, https://ebookcentral.proquest.com/lib/moore/detail.action?docID=2030868), 121–22.

one God (*heis theos*, 1 Tim. 2:5; cf. 1:17; 6:16; also Deut. 6:4, cited in the *Shema*; Rom. 3:30). This one God is the only Savior. Accordingly, there is only one salvation plan—the one that God has accomplished in Christ Jesus.[7] Now, Jew and Gentile alike can be saved and brought into personal relationship with God as *their* Savior.

God the Father

Individually and corporately those whom God saves call upon him as Father (*patēr*, 1 Tim. 1:2). There is only one reference to God as Father in each of the letters to Timothy and Titus (1 Tim. 1:2; 2 Tim. 1:2; Titus 1:4). This varies from Paul's usual style,[8] but God's fatherhood is still core to the message of each letter and is prominently stated in its opening greeting.

The title "Father" taps into a rich theological seam in all Scripture. It connotes a relationship of intimacy, familiarity, and belonging to God that has roots in the corporate old covenant notion that Yahweh was Father to his chosen people, whom he had redeemed (e.g., Ex. 4:22–23; Deut. 32:6; Hos. 1:10; 11:1), and in the messianic promises to David (2 Sam. 7:14; cf. Ps. 2:7).[9] Elsewhere in the New Testament, we read that in the *new* covenant, individual believers, Jew and Gentile, are adopted into God's family and call upon him as "Abba, Father," through their union with Christ and incorporation into his divine sonship by the renewing power of the Spirit (e.g., Matt. 6:9; John 20:17; Rom. 8:15; cf. Mark 14:36).

In 1 Timothy, the juxtaposition of "God" with Christ Jesus in several texts indicates that in those texts "God" refers to the first person of the Godhead, God *the Father* (1:1–2; 2:3, 5; 5:21; 6:13–14, cf. 3:15; 4:10).[10] This means that God *the Savior* is, in fact, God *the Father*.[11] All the other titles Paul uses for God denote God's reign over all things, but it is the

---

7   I. Howard Marshall, *The Pastoral Epistles*, ICC (Edinburgh: T&T Clark, 1999), 428–29.

8   Marshall, *Pastoral Epistles*, 104–5.

9   See Abera M. Mengestu, *God as Father in Paul: Kinship Language and Identity Formation in Early Christianity* (Eugene, OR: Wipf and Stock, 2012), 91–127.

10   See Gerald L. Bray, *The Pastoral Epistles*, ITC (London: T&T Clark, 2019), 76–78.

11   Köstenberger, *Timothy and Titus*, 148–50.

unique privilege of those whom God saves to relate to him as Savior and Father. Together with Christ Jesus, he is the source and giver to them of the salvation blessings of divine grace (*charis*), mercy (*eleos*; cf. Heb. *hesed*), and peace (*eirēnē*; cf. Heb. *shalom*, 1:2).[12]

God's fatherhood is reflected in the use of household terminology.[13] The church is "the household of God" (*oikos theou*, 1 Tim. 3:15; cf. 3:4–5), and all things are ordered by God's "household rules"[14] or "way of ordering things"[15] (*oikonomia theou*, 1:4;[16] cf. Eph. 3:2; Col. 1:25; Titus 1:7). Both concepts trade on the notion of a household where God is the head, the "heavenly *paterfamilias*,"[17] and believers have him as their Father and are to live under his rule and according to his design within the human household, the church, society, and world. He richly provides for his household in this life and the next (1 Tim. 6:17). His *benevolent* fatherhood was nothing like the fatherhood of the Greco-Roman gods and emperors who claimed the title "father" but whose capricious rule created uncertainty and fear.[18]

It is God "who gives life to all things" (6:13; cf. Gen. 1–2; Isa. 42:5). He cares and provides for his creation and determines the proper ordering and function of all things. Despite the effects of the fall, everything created by God is still "good" and "holy"—including food and marriage—and rightly received by believers with thanksgiving to God, the giver (1 Tim. 4:3–5; 6:17; cf. Gen. 1:31; Ps. 19:1–6; Rom. 1:19–20; 1 Tim. 2:15; 5:14).[19] This focus on God as Creator—his life giving, his ordered creation of Adam and Eve (1 Tim. 2:13; cf. Gen. 2), his provision of

---

12 George W. Knight, *Commentary on the Pastoral Epistles*, NIGTC (Grand Rapids, MI: Eerdmans, 1992), 66–67.

13 See chap. 4, "The Household of God."

14 Greg A. Couser, "The Sovereign Savior of 1 and 2 Timothy and Titus," in *EWTG* 112.

15 See Luke Timothy Johnson, *The First and Second Letters to Timothy*, AB 35A (New York: Doubleday, 2001), 147–54; Philip H. Towner, *The Letters to Timothy and Titus*, NICNT (Grand Rapids, MI: Eerdmans, 2006), 68–74, 112–14.

16 ESV, "stewardship from God."

17 Robert W. Wall, *1 and 2 Timothy and Titus*, THNTC (Grand Rapids, MI: Eerdmans, 2012), 178.

18 See Mengestu, *God as Father*, 71–74.

19 Bray, *Pastoral Epistles*, 220–21.

food and care (1 Tim. 2:1; 4:3–4; cf. Gen. 1:29–31; 2:8–9; oxen, 1 Tim. 5:18), and his presence in his creation (1 Tim. 2:3; 5:4, 21; 6:13; cf. Gen. 3:8)—complements the letter's message of the universal scope of salvation, and the error of the opponents' asceticism.

The Living God

The God who gives life is the "living God" (1 Tim. 4:10), and his household is "the church of the living God" (3:15). This title also has deep Old Testament roots (Deut. 5:26; Pss. 42:2; 84:2; Hos. 1:10), often in connection with the notion that God's people are to trust him as their Savior (Josh. 3:10; 1 Sam. 17:26; Dan. 4:21). Like "Savior," this title was associated with the exclusive relationship of Yahweh with Israel, but here and elsewhere in the New Testament it is recast to embrace "all people" (1 Tim. 4:10; cf. Rom. 9:25–26; 2 Cor. 3:3; Heb. 12:22).[20] Commenting on 1 Timothy 4:10, George Wieland writes, "This 'living God,' who spoke to a particular people at Sinai, made them 'children of the living God' and saved them from their enemies, is actually *sōtēr pantōn anthrōpōn*" (Savior of all people).[21]

This title would also have powerfully spoken to the life setting in Ephesus: God is not like the lifeless idols of pagan cultures (Isa. 46:5–9; Hab. 2:18–19; Acts 14:15–17; 1 Thess. 1:9) or the dead emperors, who in Ephesus were often labeled "savior."[22] The *living* God speaks (1 Tim. 4:1, 5), wills (2:4), commands (1:1), hears (2:3; 4:5), saves (2:5–6; cf. Ps. 18:46), judges (1 Tim. 2:3; 5:4), provides (4:3–4; 6:17), gives temporal and eternal life (6:13; cf. 4:8), and offers certain eternal hope (4:10). *His* temple is the church, a gathered community with whom he is a *living* presence (3:15). For Timothy and the (mostly Gentile) Ephesian Christians, who were a minority people and culture in a major center of pagan culture and worship, what comfort and encouragement it

---

20 See Wieland, *Significance*, 90–95. For discussion of the phrase "all people" in 1 Tim. 2:4 and 4:10, see below in chap. 2, "The Hope of Salvation."

21 Wieland, *Significance*, 91.

22 Abraham Kuruvilla, *1 & 2 Timothy, Titus: A Theological Commentary for Preachers* (Eugene, OR: Cascade, 2021), 92.

would have been to know that the living God, who is the only Savior for all people, was their God!

The Only God

The uniqueness and supremacy expressed in all these titles reach their peak in the two doxologies that almost bracket the letter (1 Tim. 1:17; 6:15–16), where Paul lists further divine names and attributes, piling them up to place God far above all powers and authorities, all dimensions of time, and the whole created order.[23] Again, much of the language builds upon Old Testament teaching.[24]

He is the "only" God and sovereign (1:17; 6:15). He is not *one* god among many (Ps. 86:8, 10; Isa. 37:16). There is just "*one* God" (1 Tim. 2:5; cf. Deut. 6:4).[25] He alone is ruler. This reality left no room for polytheistic claims to divine power or allegiance under the old covenant; neither does it under the new. It is an exclusive claim for devotion and worship.

God is "blessed" (*makarios*, 1 Tim. 1:11; 6:15; cf. Titus 2:13), a term not applied to God elsewhere in Scripture but common in Hellenistic Judaism.[26] He is the source and giver of all blessing, as "he contains all blessedness in himself and bestows it" on people as he chooses.[27]

He rules eternally as King (*basileus*): "King of the Ages" (1 Tim. 1:17) and "King" and "Lord" over *all* who claim or aspire to be kings and lords, whether human or spiritual (6:15; cf. Deut. 10:17; Ps. 136:3; 2 Macc. 13:4). Unlike them, he *alone* is indestructible and immortal (1 Tim. 1:17; 6:16; cf. Rom. 1:23; 1 Cor. 15:53–54), and his kingship is comprehensive, inviolable, and eternal (Ps. 10:16; Jer. 10:10; Dan. 6:26).[28] His rightful and everlasting reign over his people, over all nations, and all the earth is a consistent theme throughout Scripture (e.g.,

---

23 See Bray, *Pastoral Epistles*, 122–26.

24 Several terms are also common in Hellenistic Judaism: Towner, *Letters*, 152–53, 420–23.

25 Towner, *Letters*, 153.

26 Yarbrough, *Letters*, 118. Cf. Philo, *On the Special Laws* 1.209; 2.53; 3.1; *On the Life of Abraham* 202; *That God Is Unchangeable* 26; Josephus, *Jewish Antiquities* 10.278.

27 J. N. D. Kelly, *The Pastoral Epistles: I & II Timothy, Titus* (London: Black, 1963), 51.

28 William D. Mounce, *Pastoral Epistles*, WBC 46 (Nashville: Thomas Nelson, 2000), 61.

Ex. 15:18; 1 Sam. 8:7; Matt. 6:10; Rev. 15:3), and inseparable from his being Creator, Savior, and Judge (Pss. 24, 93, 95–99). His reign is the theological reality behind the kingdom of God preached and inaugurated by Jesus (Matt. 4:17; Mark 10:14; John 18:36; cf. 2 Sam. 7:12–16; Ps. 2) and described by Paul (Rom. 14:17; 1 Cor. 6:9–10; 15:24–25; Col. 1:13), and yet, Paul only calls God "King" in these two doxologies! God's unrivalled kingship is vital to the letter's message.

Both doxologies direct unqualified praise to God for his saving intervention in Christ Jesus (1 Tim. 1:15; 3:16; 6:13–14; cf. Rom. 16:27; 2 Cor. 1:20; Gal. 1:3–5; Phil. 4:19–20).[29] He has absolute transcendence and dwells (*oikeō*) in unapproachable light, and no eye has seen or can see him (1 Tim. 6:16; cf. Ex. 33:18–23; John 1:18; Heb. 11:27; 1 John 1:5).[30] He is also the immanent source of grace, mercy, peace, and love (1 Tim. 1:2, 14), whose saving interventions are visible in Christ's appearings, and he dwells with his people (3:15; cf. Matt. 5:8).

These lofty descriptions in the doxologies underwrite God's identity as Savior and the unrivaled certainty of his salvation plan. He cannot be seen or approached as earthly rulers are; neither is his rule subject to the dictates of time or space or mortality and death, as theirs are. He *alone* is King and Savior, worthy to receive the everlasting honor, glory (1 Tim. 1:17; cf. Rev. 4:9), and dominion that are already his (1 Tim. 6:16; cf. Ps. 96:7 [95:7 LXX]; Jude 25; Rev. 4:9, 11).[31] Little wonder Paul finishes both doxologies with "Amen," effectively asking his readers (us included) to add our voices in affirmation and praise to the one true God (cf. 1 Chron. 16:36; Neh. 8:6; Rev. 7:12).

Christ Jesus the One Mediator

In 1 Timothy, the title "Savior" is reserved for God, and Christ Jesus is the agent or means by which that salvation is accomplished, a truth wonderfully captured in one of the most succinct gospel statements in Scripture: "Christ Jesus came into the world to save sinners" (1:15).

29 Mounce, *Pastoral Epistles*, 60.
30 Mounce, *Pastoral Epistles*, 362.
31 Knight, *Pastoral Epistles*, 106, 271.

This "saying," which is "trustworthy and deserving of full acceptance," demonstrates the almost inseparable connection between Christology and soteriology in the letter, and introduces the related theme of Christ's appearings, which is a feature of all the letters to Timothy and Titus. There are four main texts about Christ (1 Tim. 1:12–15; 2:5–6; 3:16; 6:13–14). The poetic nature of some of these—and other stylized texts in the letters (e.g., 1 Tim. 1:15; 2:5; 3:16; 2 Tim. 1:9–10, 11–13; 2:19–21; 3:15; Titus 2:11–14; 3:3–7; cf. 1 Cor. 15:3–5; Phil. 2:5–11)—might indicate the use of preexisting traditional formulae or hymnic material.[32] Our interest, though, is in the meaning of the biblical text rather than its prehistory, so even if Paul did compose or use preexisting traditional material, it was to serve the message of this letter. And *that* literary context governs its meaning.

Many aspects of the teaching about Christ in the three letters are shared with Paul's other letters and the New Testament generally:[33] Christ Jesus is the God-man, who died to reconcile sinners to God, was resurrected, and ascended to reign in the heavenly places, until he comes again to bring the present age to its conclusion. Some common aspects of Paul's Christology are not explicitly mentioned (e.g., the cross [cf. 1 Tim. 6:13], divine sonship). However, Paul's letters all address specific situations, and their Christology is shaped accordingly.[34]

---

32 See Köstenberger, *Timothy and Titus*, 50–54; Linda L. Belleville, "Christology, the Pastoral Epistles, and Commentaries," in *On the Writing of New Testament Commentaries: Festschrift for Grant R. Osborne on the Occasion of His 70th Birthday*, ed. Stanley E. Porter and Eckhard J. Schnabel, TENTS 8 (Leiden: Brill, 2012), 323–35; Mounce, *Pastoral Epistles*, xcv.

33 Daniel L. Akin, "The Mystery of Godliness Is Great: Christology in the Pastoral Epistles," in *EWTG* 151–52; Gordon D. Fee, *Pauline Christology: An Exegetical-Theological Study* (Peabody, MA: Hendrickson, 2007), 472–73; Philip H. Towner, "Christology in the Letters to Timothy and Titus," in *Contours of Christology in the New Testament*, ed. Richard N. Longenecker (Grand Rapids, MI: Eerdmans, 2005), 244; Wall, *Timothy and Titus*, 164–69.

34 Eckhard J. Schnabel, "Paul, Timothy, and Titus: The Assumption of a Pseudonymous Author and of Pseudonymous Recipients in the Light of Literary, Theological, and Historical Evidence," in *Do Historical Matters Matter to Faith? A Critical Appraisal of Modern and Postmodern Approaches to Scripture*, ed. James K. Hoffmeier and Dennis R. Magary (Wheaton, IL: Crossway, 2012), 392.

The stress in 1 Timothy falls on Christ's true humanity and his historical presence in the world.[35] He is "the *man* [*anthrōpos*] Christ Jesus" (2:5), who "appeared *in the flesh*" (3:16 NIV), and "came *into the world*" (1:15; cf. Rom. 8:3–4; Gal. 4:4–5). He testified before a historical person (i.e., Pontius Pilate, 1 Tim. 6:13). He inhabited the same world as the sinners he came to save (3:16; 6:7), and because he shares our humanity, he can be a model and encouragement to Timothy (in particular) to persevere in adverse circumstances (6:12–14). Christ's physical presence in the world also affirms life in this world (2:2). Most significantly, his genuine humanity is necessary for him to be the one mediator between God and humanity (*anthrōpōn*, 2:4–5), representing us and giving himself for us in death (2:6; cf. Phil. 2:7–8; Heb. 2:14).

And yet, Christ is also divine and equal in status with God (Phil. 2:6; Col. 1:15). With God, he is the divine source of salvation blessings of grace, mercy, and peace (1 Tim. 1:2, 14, 16). With God, he commissioned and authorized Paul's apostolic ministry (1:1, 11–12; 2:7). Both God and Christ are "Lord" (*kyrios*, 1:1, 12, 14; 6:3, 14–15) and the objects of believers' hope (1:1; 4:10; 5:5; 6:17). Both are witnesses to Paul's charges to Timothy (5:21; 6:13). Christ reigns in glory (3:16).[36] His spoken words (now written) are called "Scripture" (*graphē*) and placed alongside the Mosaic Law as equally authoritative and instructive (5:18; cf. Deut. 25:4; Matt. 10:10; Luke 10:7).[37] Christ is the source of sound/healthy and authoritative teaching (1 Tim. 6:3), and of saving mercy, grace, faith, and love (1:13–14). Belief in him leads to eternal life (1:16). He receives thanks (1:12), devotion (5:11), and service (1:12; 4:6). He presently empowers Paul's gospel ministry (1:12; cf. Eph. 6:10; Phil. 4:13; 2 Tim. 2:1; 4:17). He is far superior to the angels (1 Tim. 3:16; 5:21; cf. Heb. 1:4). And in his preexistence and "coming/appearing" to accomplish *the Father's* will to save, we glimpse his divine sonship (1 Tim. 1:2; cf. Rom. 8:3; Gal. 4:4; John 5:23; 1 John 4:9, 14).

35   Towner, *Letters*, 63.
36   Akin, "Mystery," 151.
37   Knight, *Pastoral Epistles*, 234.

This is not an adoptionist Christology, where a simply human Jesus was exalted to divine status as a consequence of his earthly ministry.[38] Rather, Christ "*came* into the world" (1 Tim. 1:15) and "*appeared* in the flesh" (3:16 NIV).[39] That is, unlike us, Christ existed *before* he came into the world (John 1:1, 14; 1 Cor. 10:4; Phil. 2:6–7; Col. 1:15–17; 2 Tim. 1:10; Titus 2:11; 3:4), and his divine status *preceded* his appearing in the flesh. He is the fulfillment of God's promised salvation plan that the Messiah (Christ) would be "God with us" *and* one of us (Matt. 1:18–25; cf. Isa. 9:6–7).

Christ's appearings are a well-recognized theme of the letters to Timothy and Titus, sometimes called "epiphany Christology," after the distinctive vocabulary used (*epiphaneia*, 1 Tim. 6:14; 2 Tim. 1:10; 4:1, 8; Titus 2:13; *epiphainō*, Titus 2:11; 3:4; related word, *phaneroō*, 1 Tim. 3:16; 2 Tim. 1:10; Titus 2:11; 3:4).[40] The vocabulary denotes the appearing or revealing of what was previously hidden. It had a history of use in connection with military victories and, in secular Greek thought and Hellenistic Judaism, was associated with the visible intervention in history of otherwise invisible divine power to deliver aid.[41] Each of the three letters puts the epiphany theme to a different use, but it consistently applies to Christ's first and second appearings in history.

In 1 Timothy, this theme is also developed through related concepts, such as Christ's "coming" (1:15)[42] and the "mystery" now revealed (*mystērion*, 3:9, 16; cf. Rom. 16:25; Eph. 3:3–5; Col. 1:26).[43] The content disclosed is God's previously hidden plan of salvation. As such, Christ's appearings are both the *disclosure* of God's will to save (1 Tim. 2:4) and

38 So, classically, Hans Windisch, "Zur Christologie der Pastoralbriefe," *ZNW* 34 (1935): 213–38. See I. Howard Marshall, "The Christology of the Pastoral Epistles," *SNTSU* A 13 (1988): 159–60.
39 Andrew Y. Lau, *Manifest in the Flesh: The Epiphany Christology of the Pastoral Epistles*, WUNT 2.86 (Tübingen: Mohr Siebeck, 1996), 98–99.
40 See Towner, "Christology," 223–26.
41 Cf. LXX: 1 Chron. 17:21; 2 Macc. 2:21–23; 3:24–28; 12:22; 14:15; 15:27; Josephus, *Jewish Antiquities* 9.53–60. See Philip H. Towner, "The Present Age in the Eschatology of the Pastoral Epistles," *NTS* 32 (1986): 434–38; Lau, *Manifest in the Flesh*, 222–24.
42 Lau, *Manifest in the Flesh*, 226.
43 Yarbrough, *Letters*, 208, 220.

the *means* by which that salvation is inaugurated, accomplished, and consummated (6:14) in God's appointed timing ("the testimony," 2:6; 6:15; cf. 3:16; Titus 1:3).[44]

The centrality of Christ to every aspect of God's eternal salvation plan is captured in the Christ hymn (1 Tim. 3:16):[45] (line 1) The preexistent Christ appeared in the flesh and fulfilled his earthly ministry, climaxing in his crucifixion (6:13);[46] having satisfied God's righteous demands in his death, (line 2) he was vindicated (*edikaiōthē*) by (possibly *in*) the Holy Spirit through his resurrection from the dead (Rom. 1:4; 8:11);[47] (line 3) following his ascension, he appeared to angels (1 Tim. 5:21; cf. Eph. 1:21; Phil. 2:9–11; Heb 1:3);[48] since then, (line 4) the gospel about him is preached to the nations (1 Tim. 2:7; cf. Rom. 1:16), and (line 5) people believe on him for eternal life (1 Tim. 1:16); and (line 6) as the one taken up in glory, he now lives and reigns and intercedes for them as Lord (1:2, 12, 14; 5:21; 6:3, 13; cf. Eph. 1:20–23; Col. 3:1).[49] That is, Christ himself—"incarnate and glorified"[50]—is "the mystery of godliness."

He is the source, object, and substance of Christian "hope" (1 Tim. 1:1):[51] the (God-)man (*anthrōpos*) who is the one and only mediator (*mesitēs*) between the one God and humankind (*anthrōpōn*, 2:5), who gave himself as a ransom on behalf of and in the place of all those whom God desires to save (2:6; cf. Matt. 20:28; Mark 10:45; Gal. 1:4; Titus 2:14).

He is the Christ (*Christos*),[52] the promised Jewish Messiah (Heb. *Mashiach*) and Son of David (2 Sam. 7:8–16; Isa. 9:2–7; Rom. 1:3;

44 Couser, "Sovereign Savior," 119.
45 Commentators differ on their preferred translation and interpretation of each line—especially lines 2, 3, and 4—however, they agree that the hymn concerns the person and work of Christ, and the spread and reception of the gospel in the world. For discussion of the hymn's structure, see Mounce, *Pastoral Epistles*, 214–18.
46 Towner, *Letters*, 280.
47 Yarbrough, *Letters*, 222–23; R. Kent Hughes and Bryan Chapell, *1–2 Timothy and Titus (ESV Edition): To Guard the Deposit* (Wheaton, IL: Crossway, 2012), 86. See ESV, NIV.
48 Marshall, *Pastoral Epistles*, 526.
49 Marshall, *Pastoral Epistles*, 528–29.
50 Kelly, *Pastoral Epistles*, 90.
51 Mounce, *Pastoral Epistles*, 6.
52 1 Tim. 1:1 (2x), 2, 12, 14–16; 2:5; 3:13; 4:6; 5:11, 21; 6:3, 13–14.

2 Tim. 2:8)—but now not for Israel alone. He is Lord (*kyrios*, 1 Tim. 1:2, 12, 14; 6:3, 14). That is, he is worthy of the Greek title used to translate the divine name Yahweh in the LXX and in New Testament citations of the Old Testament (e.g., Rom. 10:16), signaling his full divinity, and yet sitting without contradiction alongside the strong monotheism of this letter and the New Testament (e.g., 1 Tim. 2:5; 1 Cor. 8:6). Paul Jeon rightly observes: "By ascribing the title 'Lord' to Christ Jesus in direct view of God the Father (1:2), Paul effectively identifies that Christ Jesus is equally the very God of the OT. Thus, Paul makes clear that Christ Jesus is the 'Lord' who shares in God the Father's position as ruler of the same household."[53] His rule will be fully realized at his second coming (1 Tim. 6:14; cf. 1 Thess. 3:13; 2 Tim. 4:1; Titus 2:13). As divine Lord, Christ Jesus is far superior to the Roman emperors, who assumed the title. He is the Lord and master of those he saves, and in this letter he is always "*our* Lord"—the personal Lord of Paul, Timothy, the Ephesian Christians, and all those who believe in him (1 Tim. 1:12–16; cf. Rom. 10:9, 13; 1 Cor. 12:3).

The Present Spirit

The Holy Spirit is mentioned twice in 1 Timothy, less frequently than some but not all of Paul's letters;[54] and common elements of Paul's pneumatology, such as the indwelling of the Spirit (e.g., 2 Tim. 1:14), do not feature. Nevertheless, the Spirit's work is integral to the message and, in keeping with the Father's desire to save and Christ Jesus's mediating role in salvation, is similarly directed toward salvation.

In the Christological and structural heart of the letter in the Christ hymn, we see that the Spirit vindicated (*edikaiōthē*, 1 Tim. 3:16; cf. Rom. 1:4) Christ through his resurrection, thereby declaring that the ransom price for sinners had been fully paid, and the demands of God's righteousness fully met in his substitutionary death (1 Tim. 2:6; cf. Rom. 1:4; 8:11).[55]

53 Paul S. Jeon, *1 Timothy: A Charge to God's Missional Household*, vol. 1 (Eugene, OR: Pickwick, 2017), 76.

54 E.g., Gal., 8.06/1000 words; Col., 1.27/1000 words; 1 Tim., 1.89/1000 words.

55 Bray, *Pastoral Epistles*, 204–5.

This same Spirit, who gave the victory to Jesus, had predicted that his followers would face setbacks and threats from people who had departed the faith (1 Tim. 4:1–3).[56] Instead of listening to the *one* Spirit (*pneuma*), who speaks clearly and truthfully (Acts 11:28; 21:11), these people would learn from liars and "deceitful spirits [*pneumasin*] and teachings of demons." *When* these warnings were spoken by the Spirit isn't specified (cf. Dan. 12:1; Mark 13:21–22; Acts 20:29–30; 2 Tim. 3:1–9),[57] but their truthfulness was confirmed by the current situation in Ephesus, which in turn certified the eschatological nature of these "later times" (i.e., the post-resurrection present).

The Spirit was the implied source of the prophecies through which Timothy was divinely appointed to his ministry (1 Tim. 1:18–20; 4:14–16; cf. 2 Tim. 1:6; Acts 20:28).[58] By extension, the Spirit would also equip and empower him to fulfill that ministry (cf. 1 Cor. 12:4–11; 1 Tim. 1:12; 2 Tim. 1:14). Similarly, the Spirit was the implied source and enabling power of Paul's unique apostolic ministry (1 Tim. 1:1, 11–16; 2:7; cf. Acts 13:2).

In short, the Spirit of God is present in the life of the church and with believers through prophetic intervention (both past and present), by which he taught, guided, and warned believers, and also identified, equipped, and empowered workers for gospel ministry.[59] Believers live in a time of spiritual conflict (1 Tim. 4:1; cf. Gal. 1:4), but it is also a time when the inbreaking of the eschatological age inaugurated in the Christ event[60] continues through the Spirit's ministry. Regardless of the circumstances or threats, and no matter how long before Christ's second appearing, God's plan of salvation is being advanced by his Spirit, and nothing can prevent its consummation.

---

56 Jerome D. Quinn, "The Holy Spirit in the Pastoral Epistles," in *Sin, Salvation and the Spirit*, ed. D. Durken (Collegeville, MN: Liturgical Press, 1979), 357.

57 Mounce, *Pastoral Epistles*, 234.

58 Towner, *Letters*, 156.

59 See Michael A. G. Haykin, "The Fading Vision? The Spirit and Freedom in the Pastoral Epistles," *EvQ* 57 (1985): 291–305.

60 I will use the summary term "Christ event" to refer to the person and work of Christ in salvation—his incarnation, earthly ministry, crucifixion, resurrection, ascension, and (where applicable) glorious return.

The Triune God Who Saves

God's person and work are key to the message of 1 Timothy. The one God has just one plan of salvation for all people, and the letter portrays the three divine persons performing different roles with the single purpose to accomplish that salvation in the past, present, and eschatological future. The universal supremacy of God our Savior, the full divinity and humanity of Christ Jesus, and the all-knowing, vindicating power of the Spirit ensure that no human or spiritual force can prevent God's plan from being realized, and so they provide Timothy and all believers with certainty and urgency to join in God's saving agenda.

2

The Hope of Salvation

IF GOD IS THE PRIMARY INTEREST of 1 Timothy, the primary interest of God in 1 Timothy is salvation. This is conveyed in many ways but is readily apparent in the threefold designation of God as Savior (1:1; 2:3; 4:10) and Christ Jesus's role as the one mediator and means of salvation (1:1, 15; 2:5–6; 3:16). It's also evident in Paul's divine commissioning as apostle and preacher of the gospel (1:1, 11–16; 2:7) and the urgency of Timothy's task to silence false teachers (1:3, 18; 6:2–5), instill proper church leadership (2:8–3:15; 5:17–22), teach sound doctrine, and model the godly life (4:6–16; 6:11–14). The chief purpose of the letter is to advance and protect God's purpose and plan of salvation, and accordingly, "the language and ideas of salvation are pervasive," as they are in 2 Timothy and Titus.[1]

Who Needs to Be Saved?

Those who need to be saved are "sinners" (*hamartōloi*, 1 Tim. 1:15), and sin is the reason they need to be saved. We see how sin is manifest in human lives in two vice lists (1:9–10; 6:3–5) and other proscribed behaviors; and while the picture is not exhaustive, sin's destructive effect on individual lives and relationships, especially our relationship with God, is clear.

---

1   George M. Wieland, "The Function of Salvation in the Letters to Timothy and Titus," in *EWTG* 153.

There are

- *attitudinal* sins: anger (2:8), vanity (2:9), pride (3:6), and envy (6:4);
- sins of *speech*: lying (1:10), quarrelling (2:8; 6:4), being double-tongued (3:8), gossip and saying what should not be said (5:13), and slander (6:4); and
- sins involving the wrongful *use of the body and material world*: sexual sins (1:10), immodesty and extravagance (2:9), excessive use of alcohol (3:3, 8; cf. 5:23), rejecting the good gifts of creation (4:3), overindulgence in pleasure (5:6), greed, and love and worship of money and possessions (2:9; 3:3, 8; 6:5, 9–10, 17).

Some sins plainly deny the equal humanity, dignity, and welfare of others (e.g., murder and violence, 1:9; 3:3) or objectify them for financial gain (the sins of "enslavers," 1:10). Some is so consuming and habitual, it defines those who practice it (e.g., "the sexually immoral," "liars," 1:10). Some sins are publicly known; others are revealed later (5:24). Most sins mentioned are sins of commission, but sins of omission are implied, such as disrespect and dishonor (5:1–3, 8, 11–12, 17; 6:2).

However, sin isn't confined to human relationships and the world of things. Some sin is deliberately Godward. As in Old Testament times, there are those who offer unacceptable and idolatrous worship and flagrantly reject God's rule and law (1:9–10; cf. Ex. 20:12–16; 21:12–16).[2] God's law was, in fact, laid down for such people.[3] But the capacity of humans to oppose God and do evil is limitless, as the catchall phrase "whatever else is contrary to sound doctrine" indicates.[4] All sin, whether it is named in the Decalogue or not, is

---

2   See Dillon Thornton, "Sin Seizing an Opportunity through the Commandments," *HBT* 36 (2014): 142–58.

3   Stephen Westerholm, "The Law and the 'Just Man' (1 Tim. 1:3–11)," *ST* 36 (1982): 84–85.

4   Thornton, "Sin Seizing an Opportunity," 155.

against God and his gospel standard.[5] Some people, once including Paul, blaspheme against God and his gospel, denying and defaming him (1 Tim. 1:13, 20; 6:1, 4). Some forbid things he has given as good gifts (4:3–4). And some damage God's household through false teaching (1:6), persecution and opposition (1:13), and conduct causing reputational harm (3:7).

Yet, as morally abhorrent as some of these sins would have been even to those outside the church,[6] individual sins are not the main issue. It is that those who sin are *sinners*, and while there is scope for repentance and change (1:3, 13–14; 5:1, 20; 6:17)—even rehabilitation (1:20), progress (4:15), and good works (2:10; 5:10, 25; 6:18)—one *remains* a "sinner redeemed"[7] (1:15, present tense: "I *am* the foremost").

And the list of sinners—those already saved and those in need of salvation—is expansive. The word "sinners" denotes not just Gentiles (Gal. 2:15) or Jews who did not keep the Mosaic law in certain ways, as the label had historically been applied,[8] but also Jewish Paul (1 Tim. 1:15); Timothy, with Jewish-Gentile ancestry; and "all people," including Gentiles (2:4, 7; 4:10); women and men (2:8–15; 5:1–2, 9–16); old and young (5:1–2); married and widowed (3:1–12; 5:3); kings and all in high positions (2:2); slaves and masters (6:1–2); wealthy and otherwise (6:17); faithful and erring church leaders and false teachers (1:3–7, 19–20; 5:17, 20; 6:20–21); and the congregation itself (6:21).

As Scripture consistently affirms, *all* people are sinners (Ps. 14:1–3; Rom. 3:23), for we are all descended from Adam and Eve, who sinned and became sinners, albeit by different paths (1 Tim. 2:14; cf. Gen. 3). For all the "law's undoubted glories," it cannot change this (1 Tim. 1:7–10; cf. Rom. 7; 2 Cor. 3:7).[9] Christ Jesus alone is without sin (Heb. 4:15; 1 Pet. 3:18).

---

5   William D. Mounce, *Pastoral Epistles*, WBC 46 (Nashville: Thomas Nelson, 2000), 40–41.
6   I. Howard Marshall, *The Pastoral Epistles*, ICC (Edinburgh: T&T Clark, 1999), 378.
7   Gordon D. Fee, *1 and 2 Timothy, Titus*, NIBC (Peabody, MA: Hendrickson, 1988), 53.
8   Michael F. Bird, "Sin, Sinner," in *DJG* 1944.
9   Robert W. Yarbrough, *The Letters to Timothy and Titus*, PNTC (Grand Rapids, MI: Eerdmans, 2018), 125.

From What Are They Saved?

Rebellion against God is not just a feature of human lives. First Timothy testifies to spiritual opposition. Satan (*satanas*) holds sway over a realm outside the household of God and gives rise to blasphemous false teaching, scandal, and apostasy (1:20; 5:14–15). The devil (*diabolos*)[10] can snare believers, especially leaders (3:6–7; 6:9; cf. 2 Tim. 2:26). Deceitful spirits and demons are the source of false teaching (1 Tim. 4:1). The mention of Eve being deceived (2:14) recalls the serpent, whose trickery was "ultimately the voice of Satan" (see Gen. 3:4, 13; 2 Cor. 11:3).[11]

But none of this poses a threat to God's plan or rule. The Holy Spirit had forewarned that demonic teaching would arise in later times (1 Tim. 4:1). The devil's snares can be avoided through godly maturity and contentment (3:6–7; 6:6–7). Satan can even be used by God as a pedagogical tool to bring about repentance (1:19–20; cf. 1 Cor. 5:5)! That is, while evil spiritual beings are a feature of the present age, they are totally subject to God (1 Tim. 6:15–16; cf. Job 2:6; Rom. 16:20; Col. 2:15). The faithful need not be ensnared. God's salvation holds for those who repent and believe (1 Tim. 1:13), and who persevere in faith and godly living (2:15; cf. 2 Tim. 2:25–26). He will preserve his people from such dangers.

Nevertheless, judgment for all people is a present (1 Tim. 1:13; 3:6; 5:12, 21; 6:13; cf. Ps. 82) and future reality (1 Tim. 5:12; 6:9; cf. Acts 10:42; 2 Tim. 4:1, 8). Everything will be weighed, from public sins and the secrets of hearts (1 Tim. 5:24; cf. 1 Cor. 4:5), to "good works" that are known or hidden (1 Tim. 5:25; cf. Rev. 14:13). God is the judge. He is watching (1 Tim. 2:3; 5:4, 21; 6:13), and he decides what is "good" (*kalos*, 1:8, 18; 2:3; 3:1; 4:4, 6; 5:10, 25; 6:12, 18; *agathos*, 1:5, 19; 2:10; 5:10; cf. 6:18) and what pleases him (2:3; 5:4).[12]

---

10 "Satan" and "the devil" are used interchangeably in the New Testament, e.g., Matt. 4:10–11.

11 Kenneth Mathews, *Genesis 1–11:26: An Exegetical and Theological Exposition of Holy Scripture*, NAC (Nashville: B&H, 1996), 234.

12 See Marshall, *Pastoral Epistles*, 227–29.

The just penalty of sin is death, and so sinners need to be saved from this eschatological "ruin and destruction"[13] (6:9; cf. Gen. 2:17; 2 Thess. 1:9; 1 Tim. 5:6). This is the certain hope found in God's salvation plan: "eternal *life*" (1 Tim. 1:16; 4:8; 6:12, 19; cf. Rom. 5:21; 6:23).

How Are They Saved?

Salvation belongs to God: God is our Savior, *the* Savior (1 Tim. 1:1; 2:3; 4:10), and Christ Jesus is both the revelation of God's plan to save and the one through whom it is realized. His coming into the world (1:15), incarnation, earthly life and ministry, condemnation by authorities (6:13), death, resurrection, and ascension (3:16)[14] were all to save sinners. Indeed, God's way of ordering all things is centered on his salvation plan in the gospel (1:4, 11).

In Scripture, the first promise of Christ's coming occurs immediately after our first parents sinned, in the Lord God's judgment and curse on the serpent (Gen. 3:15). God put enmity between the serpent and the woman it had deceived, and between its offspring and hers (Heb. *zera'*, "seed"). The woman's offspring would bruise the serpent's head, and the serpent would bruise his heel. This so-called *protevangelium* is the first glimpse of God's promised salvation that is ultimately fulfilled in Christ. *He* is the promised chosen seed, born of woman (Gal. 3:16; 4:4), who in his death overcame Satan and all the consequences of the fall (Rom. 16:20; Heb. 2:14).[15]

It is *this* "childbearing" (*tēs teknogonias*) that some interpreters consider Paul has in mind in 1 Tim. 2:15, so that the verse means that, notwithstanding her part in the fall (2:14), Eve (and all women) can/will be saved by the messianic child born to Mary.[16] The verse *is*

13 Mounce, *Pastoral Epistles*, 345; Philip H. Towner, *The Letters to Timothy and Titus*, NICNT (Grand Rapids, MI: Eerdmans, 2006), 403.
14 See lines 1, 2, 3, and 6 of the Christ hymn.
15 See Mathews, *Genesis*, 245–48.
16 So, George W. Knight, *Commentary on the Pastoral Epistles*, NIGTC (Grand Rapids, MI: Eerdmans, 1992), 144–47; Ben Witherington III, *A Socio-Rhetorical Commentary on Titus, 1–2 Timothy and 1–3 John*, vol. 1 of *Letters and Homilies for Hellenized Christians* (Downers Grove, IL: InterVarsity, 2006), ProQuest Ebook Central, https://ebookcentral

difficult to understand, and this interpretation is possible. However, I am not persuaded by this view. While what it claims is true and has the benefit of maintaining the link with Genesis 2–3, which feature in the instructions about the ministry of women in the public assembly (1 Tim. 2:11–14), if Paul had in mind Jesus's birth, this would be a very obscure way of making the point,[17] and lexical, grammatical, and contextual factors argue against it.[18]

The one who came into the world to save sinners is "the man Christ Jesus," who is the "one mediator [*mesitēs*] between God and men" (2:5). Mediators are needed when there is a breach in relationship; they go between two parties and bridge the gap to bring reconciliation and restoration of relationship. The breach between God and humanity is the result of sin. All people (except Jesus) are sinners who cannot be in the presence of the holy God (Ps. 24:3–4), and so in this regard Christ is uniquely qualified to mediate for us in God's presence. As the *one* mediator, "Christ alone is able to deal with God on behalf of humankind, and the salvation thereby provided is available to all"; he far surpasses all other mediators of God's covenant—from angels to Moses (see Ps. 106:23; Gal. 3:19; Heb. 3:1–6; 8:6).[19]

Some may wonder if "men" and "man" in 1 Timothy 2:5 excludes women or lessens Christ's identification with women. Not at all! What we can miss in our English Bibles is that in this chapter Paul uses two

.proquest.com/lib/moore/detail.action?docID=2030868, 259–60; Linda L. Belleville, "1 Timothy," in *1 Timothy, 2 Timothy, Titus, Hebrews*, ed. Philip W. Comfort, CBC 17 (Carol Stream, IL: Tyndale, 2009), 56, 62–63; also RSV footnote.

17 Donald Guthrie, *The Pastoral Epistles*, TNTC (1957; repr., Leicester: Inter-Varsity Press, 1984), 78.

18 See Thomas R. Schreiner, "An Interpretation of 1 Timothy 2:9–15: A Dialogue with Scholarship," in *Women in the Church: An Interpretation and Application of 1 Timothy 2:9–15*, 3rd ed., ed. Andreas J. Köstenberger and Thomas R. Schreiner (Wheaton, IL: Crossway, 2016), 216–24; Andreas J. Köstenberger, "Ascertaining Women's God-Ordained Roles: An Interpretation of 1 Timothy 2:15," *BBR* 7 (1997): 107–44.

19 See George Wieland, *The Significance of Salvation: A Study of Salvation Language in the Pastoral Epistles*, PBM (Milton Keynes, UK: Paternoster, 2006), 58–63 (quoting p. 62); Jerome D. Quinn and W. C. Wacker, *The First and Second Letters to Timothy: A New Translation with Notes and Commentary*, ECC (Grand Rapids, MI: Eerdmans, 2000), 165–66, 182–86.

different words, both of which can be rendered "man." He uses the generic term *anthrōpos* for Jesus *and* for humanity (men and women; 2:1, 4–5; 4:10), before switching to the gendered term *anēr* to discuss men's conduct (2:8) as distinct from that of women (2:9). As such, the use of *anthrōpos* in 2:5 highlights both the *shared* humanity of men and women and that this *same* humanity was taken on by Christ. Christ is truly human. He is also truly divine. He is therefore uniquely qualified to be the mediator between God and humanity.[20]

Christ mediates salvation by giving himself as a ransom (*antilytron*) for all (2:6). In Jesus's own words, he came "to give his life as a ransom [*lytron*] for [*anti*] many" (Mark 10:45; cf. Titus 2:14). The concept of ransom is that of paying a price to obtain freedom.[21] It is the language of the slave market. For Jewish hearers it recalled Yahweh's great act of redemption in delivering Israel from slavery and death in Egypt (Ex. 6:6; Deut. 7:8), but the message of Scripture is that *all* people are held in bondage to sin and death (John 8:34; Rom. 6:17, 23), and are utterly incapable of paying God the cost of their redemption (Ps. 49:7–9; Mark 8:37). Someone else must pay our ransom price.

Leon Morris concludes his classic study of the *lytron* word group, by observing that in the New Testament

it is a metaphor which involves the payment of a price which is plainly stated in several places and understood in others to be the death of Christ. From the very nature of the imagery this involves a substitutionary idea; instead of our death there is His, instead of our slavery there is His blood.[22]

Here in 1 Timothy 2:6, Christ's self-offering for those he saves is *both* sub-stitutionary (*anti*, "instead of") *and* representative (*hyper*, "for/on behalf of"). He paid the price in every way necessary to secure our freedom.

<hr>

20 See Gerald L. Bray, *The Pastoral Epistles*, ITC (London: T&T Clark, 2019), 151–56.
21 See Leon Morris, *The Apostolic Preaching of the Cross* (Grand Rapids, MI: Eerdmans, 1965), 11–53.
22 Morris, *Apostolic Preaching*, 53.

Moreover, he is both priest and sacrifice, in that he *gave* (*didōmi*) himself and he gave *himself* (Gal. 1:4; cf. Rev. 5:9).[23] In doing so, he fulfilled and surpassed the sacrificial system and priesthood of the old covenant (Lev. 4; Heb. 9:12–14, 24–26). Christ, the sinless perfect man, interceded as the one mediator between God and men, giving himself in our place as the perfect and acceptable sacrifice for sins to ransom us for God and secure eternal redemption.[24] He is the suffering servant promised in Isaiah 53:11–12: the righteous, chosen servant of the Lord, who sacrificed himself to bear the guilt of many. And having secured forgiveness of sins in his flesh, he has been vindicated by God in the Spirit through his resurrection from the dead (1 Tim. 3:16). In God's saving plan, *this* is the "testimony [*martyrion*] given at the proper time" (2:6) that reveals, accomplishes, and testifies to God's desire to save all people and, accordingly, is the gospel Paul is to preach to the Gentiles (2:7; cf. 1:11).[25]

A person is saved and receives eternal life by believing (*pisteuō*, 1:16; 3:16; 4:10) in Christ and his saving work. Importantly, it is not the *experience* of faith that saves but the *object* of that faith (i.e., Christ, 2:5–6; 3:16); hence, the stress on "truth" and "sound words" over against the message of the false teachers (6:3–5), and the reason why, as "agents of God's salvation,"[26] Paul and his coworkers strive to make the gospel known (4:10; cf. 1:18; 6:12; Col. 1:29). To be saved is, in fact, to "come to the knowledge of the truth" (1 Tim. 2:4; cf. 2 Tim. 2:24; 3:7; Titus 1:1):[27] not mere intellectual assent but a sinner's *personal relationship* of complete trust and reliance upon Christ (*ep' autō*, 1 Tim. 1:16),[28] leading to comprehensive conversion of thought and life (e.g., 1:5, 19;

23 Wieland, *Significance*, 62.
24 See Philip H. Towner, *The Goal of Our Instruction: The Structure of Theology and Ethics in the Pastoral Epistles*, JSNTSup 34 (Sheffield: JSOT, 1989), 83–87.
25 Knight, *Pastoral Epistles*, 124; S. M. Baugh, " 'Savior of All People': 1 Tim. 4:10 in Context," *WTJ* 54 (1992): 339.
26 Wieland, "Function of Salvation," 158.
27 Wieland, *Significance*, 55.
28 Murray J. Harris, *Prepositions and Theology in the Greek New Testament: An Essential Reference Resource for Exegesis* (Grand Rapids, MI: Zondervan, 2012), 235.

3:9; 4:8).[29] At no point does this change; one must persevere in faith and godliness (2:15; 4:16; cf. Matt. 10:22).

Salvation has past, present, and future dimensions.[30] References to the "proper time" point to the past plan of God being realized in the present and future (1 Tim. 2:6; 6:15). God's desire to save is a present and ongoing reality (2:4). The receipt of salvation is a past and present experience for those who believe in Christ (1:15–16). God has called Timothy to eternal life (6:13). The need to be preserved from error and persevere in salvation has eschatological salvation in view. The theme of "hope," which is focused on "Christ Jesus our hope," is ultimately met eschatologically (1:1; 4:10; 6:17–19; cf. 5:5; Titus 1:2).[31] And while the concept of "life" (*zōē*) is a future (eternal) reality (1 Tim. 4:8; 6:12, 19), believers even now have a "heightened enjoyment of the things of this life" through their knowledge of the truth and dependence on God (4:3–5, 8; 5:5; 6:17; cf. John 10:10).[32]

Who Is Saved?

Sinners are saved. But which sinners? Certainly not all. If they were, there would be no reason for the letter. As it is, 1 Timothy is urgent in its concern to prevent false teaching (1:3), promote and preserve the gospel and sound teaching, ensure the church exists as the "pillar and buttress of truth" (3:15), and prevent people from being ensnared by the devil and ruin (1:20; 3:6–7; 4:1; 5:14–15; 6:9–10). Moreover, those who believe (*pisteuō*/*pistos*, 1:16; 4:3, 10, 12; 5:16; 6:2) in Christ are saved (1:15–16), and therefore the *un*believing (*apistos*, 1:13; 5:8; cf. Titus 1:15) are not.

And yet there are statements that seem to pull in the other direction: prayers for *all* people (*pantōn anthrōpōn*) please God, "who desires *all* people [*pantas anthrōpous*] to be saved" (1 Tim. 2:1–4); the one

---

29 See Towner, *Goal*, 249–56.

30 Mounce, *Pastoral Epistles*, cxxxii; Andreas J. Köstenberger, *Commentary on 1–2 Timothy and Titus*, BTCP (Nashville: Holman Reference, 2017), 439–40.

31 See Wieland, *Significance*, 28–33.

32 Wieland, *Significance*, 103.

mediator between God and men "gave himself as a ransom for *all*" (*pas*, 2:5–6); and God is "the Savior of *all* people" (*pantōn anthrōpōn*, 4:10).

A full discussion of divine love and sovereignty, election, predestination, and free will—the truths behind this apparent tension—lies beyond this study. However, there are pointers toward a resolution:[33]

1. The letter addresses a heresy that seems to have involved restricting salvation to certain people, so we can expect pushback to correct such exclusivist thinking.

2. The heresy denied the salvation-historical development of the gospel, whereby God's intention to save all nations (Ps. 67:2; Isa. 52:10) had been realized in Christ, and the blessings that were Israel's were now for the nations (Gal. 3:14).

3. In fact, God's ordering of *all* things (*oikonomia theou*, 1 Tim. 1:4)[34] is directed toward his desire that all people would be saved, and so the letter stresses the universal scope of salvation through themes such as the oneness of God (1:17; 2:5; 6:15), the one mediator (2:5), Paul's apostleship to the Gentiles (1:1; 2:7), Christ's being proclaimed "among the nations" and believed on "in the world" (3:16), believers meeting "in every place" (2:8; cf. Mal. 1:11; 1 Cor. 1:2), and "kings and those in high positions" being the focus of prayer (1 Tim. 2:1). The point is not that God saves all people (i.e., universalism) but that his salvation embraces all kinds or categories of people, not just ethnic Israel (Matt. 28:19). Salvation is for every person *without distinction*, not every person without exception.[35]

4. So in 1 Tim. 4:10, where God is "the Savior of all people, especially of those who believe," Paul is not contrasting two notions of salvation: one referring to God's common grace provision for all people and another enjoyed by a subset of those who receive material *and*

---

33 Köstenberger, *Timothy and Titus*, 438–39.

34 See chap. 4, "The Household of God."

35 See Thomas R. Schreiner, " 'Problematic Texts' for Definite Atonement in the Pastoral and General Epistles," in *From Heaven He Came and Sought Her: Definite Atonement in Historical, Biblical, Theological, and Pastoral Perspective*, ed. David Gibson and Jonathan Gibson (Wheaton, IL: Crossway, 2013), 376–87.

spiritual blessings (i.e., believers).[36] Rather, God is identified as the *only* source of salvation for all people, and those who receive his salvation are *those who believe*.[37] The same pattern is found in 2:4.

5. God does not want any to perish and shows abundant patience to those in need of salvation (1:16; cf. Rom. 2:4; 2 Pet. 3:9); and he is pleased by evangelistically motivated prayers for all people (1 Tim. 2:1–3).[38]

6. Salvation is based on God's initiative and choice (6:12; cf. Rom. 8:30; 2 Tim. 1:9); and it is God who answers prayers that provide conditions conducive to the spread of the gospel (1 Tim. 2:1–3; cf. Jer. 29:7; Col. 4:3).[39]

7. Salvation is a gift of superabundant grace (1 Tim. 1:14), as those in need of saving are utterly incapable of achieving or securing their own salvation.

Therein lay the danger of the false teachers. Their teaching had elitist elements that likely restricted salvation to certain people on the basis of myths and genealogies, and it was contrary to faith, as it promoted speculative interpretations of the Old Testament and Jewish law, and demanded asceticism (1:4, 7; 4:3, 7; cf. 2 Tim. 4:4; Titus 1:14; 3:9).[40] God's salvation, however, is by faith and available to all (1 Tim. 1:4; 2:4).

Paul as a Pattern of a Saved Sinner

In both Testaments, the deliverance of Israel from Egypt functions as a paradigm of God's saving will and deeds (e.g., Mic. 7:15–17; 1 Cor. 10; Jude 5). Here, Paul's own receipt and experience of God's salvation provide a pattern for those who would also believe in Christ.

First, Paul is the foremost of sinners; the prototype of those who need to be saved (1 Tim. 1:15). Even though he is a Jew versed in the law (Acts

---

36 So, Baugh, "Savior of All People," 331.

37 Schreiner, "Problematic Texts," 385–86.

38 William B. Barcley, "1 Timothy," in *BTINT* 363–64.

39 Towner, *Goal*, 203.

40 Fee, *Timothy, Titus*, 7–10, 62, 64.

22:3; Gal. 1:14), he is not one of "the just" but one of those for whom the law was laid down—a "sinner" and "blasphemer" (1 Tim. 1:13, 15; cf. 1:20), who violently persecuted believers (1:13; cf. Acts 9:4; 1 Cor. 15:9). He was an enemy of God acting in ignorant unbelief, like those who crucified Jesus (Luke 23:34),[41] like the Gentiles (1 Thess. 4:5), *and like Israel* (Rom. 10:3, 14).[42] He could contribute nothing to his salvation but was shown mercy by God (*ēleēthēn*, 1 Tim. 1:13, 16; cf. Rom. 11:30–31; 1 Tim. 1:2), even being appointed to gospel ministry! He is proof that Jew and Gentile alike need to be saved by faith and that no one is beyond the reach of Christ's mercy and grace.

Second, Christ's patience and mercy toward Paul serves as a pattern (*hypotypōsin*) given *by Christ* for those who would also believe on Christ (1 Tim. 1:16). Paul's experience testifies to the efficacy of the gospel he preaches and is a demonstration of and advertisement for the unlimited extent of Christ's mercy and patience to realize God's desire to save.[43]

Third, Paul provides a model of faithful, gospel-focused ministry as the fitting response to divine grace, first to Timothy (1:2, 18; cf. 1 Cor. 4:17; 2 Tim. 3:10–11), but also to all who are saved. That's not to say all believers are to be exactly like him. His ministry is unique as a herald, apostle, and trailblazer of the mission to the Gentiles (1 Tim. 1:1, 16; 2:7; cf. 2 Tim. 1:11; Titus 1:3). His ministry is itself part of God's plan of salvation. Nevertheless, Paul's life-transforming reception of the gospel and faithful ministry provide a model from which Timothy and all others can learn. Christ is (to be) proclaimed among the nations by many more than just Paul (1 Tim. 3:16)!

Finally, Paul's palpable amazement and gratitude in response to Christ's superabundant grace provide a model for all similarly undeserving recipients of such a great salvation.[44] The doxology is a joyous outburst of praise to God, the giver (1:17).

41 J. N. D. Kelly, *The Pastoral Epistles: I & II Timothy, Titus* (London: Black, 1963), 53.
42 Wieland, *Significance*, 41–2.
43 Marshall, *Pastoral Epistles*, 401–3; Wieland, *Significance*, 45.
44 Kelly, *Pastoral Epistles*, 52.

3

The Word of God

AT THE HEART OF THE THREAT to the church in Ephesus was an attack against the word of God. The threat of the false teachers was not just their conduct or methods (1 Tim. 1:6–7, 19; 4:1–2; 6:4–5, 20). It was that they taught different doctrine (1:3; 6:3) that was opposed to the gospel and sound teaching.[1] It was a contest for truth, and they were deceived liars, "deprived of the truth" (4:1–2; 6:5), doing the work of "the father of lies" (John 8:44). But God's word and God's work are about the truth, knowledge of which leads to salvation (1 Tim. 2:4).

The Apostolic Message

Paul uses several terms for the fixed body of orthodox content to be believed, protected, preserved, proclaimed, and taught by and among believers. The different terms highlight different aspects of the apostolic message, but their overlapping nature means that rigid distinctions regarding their content or intended audience or associated verbs for speech are misguided.[2]

---

1 See Gerald L. Bray, *The Pastoral Epistles*, ITC (London: T&T Clark, 2019), 282–84.
2 See Claire Smith, "'Preaching': Toward Lexical Clarity for Better Practice," in *Theology Is for Preaching: Biblical Foundations, Method, and Practice*, ed. Chase R. Kuhn and Paul Grimmond (Bellingham, WA: Lexham, 2021), 34–52.

"The Faith"

"Faith" terminology is a feature of the letters to Timothy and Titus, especially 1 Timothy.[3] The verb occurs twice for active belief in Christ and the gospel (1:16; 3:16). But the noun (*pistis*) occurs nineteen times! It is used in three senses: (1) for the fixed body of orthodox content that is the subject of Paul's preaching and teaching (2:7),[4] "the mystery" about Christ (3:9; cf. 3:16), which can be believed and learned (3:9, 13; 4:6; 6:12) or rejected (1:19; 4:1; 5:8; 6:10, 21); (2) for subjective faith/ trust in Christ (1:5, 14, 19; 2:15; 5:12; cf. *pisteuō*, 1:16; 3:16); and (3) in a combined sense, for the sphere of new life that comes from belief in Christ and orthodox teaching (1:2, 4; 4:12).[5] The use of this term for the body of content *and* for personal belief in Christ and that same content, *and* for the new life that issues from them, draws attention to the operation of God's plan, which is *by faith* (1:4). By contrast, the false teachers promoted myths, genealogies, speculation, and ascetic observances.

"The Truth"

"The truth" (*alētheia*) likewise refers to the apostolic gospel and full body of orthodox doctrine, but adds a qualitative assessment by identifying it as the genuine revelation of God, and thus free from lies and falsehood (Titus 1:2),[6] and in doing so highlights the falsehood of other truth claims (Gal. 2:5; 5:7).[7] To be saved is to "come to the knowledge of the truth" (1 Tim. 2:4; cf. 2 Tim. 2:25; 3:7; Titus 1:1; Heb. 10:26).[8] Paul preached "faith and truth" (1 Tim. 2:7).[9] The church is "a pillar

---

3   See I. Howard Marshall, *The Pastoral Epistles*, ICC (Edinburgh: T&T Clark, 1999), 214–17; William D. Mounce, *Pastoral Epistles*, WBC 46 (Nashville: Thomas Nelson, 2000), cxxx–cxxxii.
4   Gordon D. Fee, *1 and 2 Timothy, Titus*, NIBC (Peabody, MA: Hendrickson, 1988), 67.
5   Philip H. Towner, *The Letters to Timothy and Titus*, NICNT (Grand Rapids, MI: Eerdmans, 2006), 100.
6   See Marshall, *Pastoral Epistles*, 122–23.
7   Philip H. Towner, *The Goal of Our Instruction: The Structure of Theology and Ethics in the Pastoral Epistles*, JSNTSup 34 (Sheffield: JSOT, 1989), 122.
8   See George Wieland, *The Significance of Salvation: A Study of Salvation Language in the Pastoral Epistles*, PBM (Milton Keynes, UK: Paternoster, 2006), 56.
9   Fee, *Timothy, Titus*, 67.

and buttress of the truth," which it is to maintain, protect, and serve[10] (3:15). Those who "believe and know the truth" live rightly in God's creation (4:3), but false teachers are "deprived of the truth" (6:5).

"Teaching"

The vocabulary of "teaching" is also a feature of the letters to Timothy and Titus. The noun (*didaskalia*) appears more often than in any other New Testament book.[11] In 1 Timothy, it refers to the activity of authoritative teaching (4:13, 16; 5:17; cf. 2 Tim. 3:10, 16; Titus 2:7), and the body of content/doctrine authorized by God that was taught (1 Tim. 1:10–11; 6:1; cf. Titus 2:10),[12] which is "sound" (1 Tim. 1:10; cf. 2 Tim. 4:3; Titus 1:9; 2:7), is "good" (1 Tim. 4:6), and "accords with godliness" (6:3). It includes both theological and ethical content.[13] The prominence of teaching terminology signals the key role of learning in the Christian life and the church. Notably, the opponents also used educational means to advance their agenda, but they "taught *different doctrine*" (*heterodidaskaleō*, 1:3; 6:3), aspired to be "teachers of the *law*" (*nomodidaskaloi*, 1:7), and were devoted to "*teachings* of demons" (4:1; note *plural*). This is why they must be stopped (1:3).

"The Gospel"

The word "gospel" occurs only once (1:11; cf. 2 Tim. 1:8, 10; 2:8; 4:5), which is unexpected in a letter so concerned with salvation. The term itself (*euangelion*) focuses attention on both the communication of content and its quality, in that this is a message of *good* news to be *announced*. As "the gospel of the glory of the blessed God," it has its origins with God, belongs to him, and is about his glory[14] (see 2 Cor. 4:4, 6). It is the message of salvation by which people are saved and is the theological core of God's plan[15] and thus the basis and measure of

10 Marshall, *Pastoral Epistles*, 511.
11 1 Tim. (8x); 2 Tim. (3x); Titus (4x).
12 Mounce, *Pastoral Epistles*, 42.
13 Towner, *Goal*, 123.
14 Mounce, *Pastoral Epistles*, 43; Fee, *Timothy, Titus*, 47.
15 Greg A. Couser, "The Sovereign Savior of 1 and 2 Timothy and Titus," in *EWTG* 112.

all authentic apostolic doctrine and paraenesis (1 Tim. 1:10–11). It was entrusted to Paul by God and is the reason for his apostleship (1:11; cf. Rom. 1:16–17; 1 Tim. 2:7; 2 Tim. 2:8). In the same vein, Paul was also appointed a herald/preacher (*kēryx*, 1 Tim. 2:7; 2 Tim. 1:11), and Christ is "proclaimed [*kēryssō*] among the nations" (1 Tim. 3:16; cf. *kērygma*, Rom. 16:25; 1 Cor. 1:21; 2 Tim. 4:17; Titus 1:3).

Further Terms

Other terms highlight further aspects of the apostolic message. As "mystery" (*mystērion*), it is truth that had been hidden and unknowable but has now been revealed by God through the appearing of Christ in history (1 Tim. 3:9, 16; cf. Rom. 16:25; Eph. 3:4).[16] As the "deposit" (*parathēkē*, 1 Tim. 6:20; also 2 Tim. 1:12, 14)—a term not found elsewhere in the New Testament—it implies a process of transmission, with a stress on the *value* of what is entrusted and the need to preserve and care for it into the future (2 Tim. 2:2).[17] As "words" (*logoi*), the message possesses a verbal and propositional nature (1 Tim. 4:6); "the sound words of our Lord" rejected by the opponents (6:3) are words *about* Christ in the apostolic gospel (see 1 Thess. 1:8) and teaching that comes *from* and is *authorized* by him.[18] There's also the prophetic speech of the Spirit (1 Tim. 4:1; cf. 1:18; 4:14).

The "faithful/trustworthy saying" formula (*pistos ho logos*, 1:15; 3:1; 4:9; cf. 2 Tim. 2:11; Titus 3:8) is unique to the letters to Timothy and Titus[19] and emphasizes the truthfulness, reliability, significance, and authority of certain propositions.[20] Twice in 1 Timothy, the formula is strengthened with the additional commendation of being "deserving

---

16 Marshall, *Pastoral Epistles*, 490, 523.

17 Towner, *Letters*, 430–31.

18 Dillon T. Thornton, *Hostility in the House of God: An Investigation of the Opponents in 1 and 2 Timothy*, BBRSup 15 (Winona Lake, IN: Eisenbrauns, 2016), 72–73.

19 Ben Witherington III, *A Socio-Rhetorical Commentary on Titus, 1–2 Timothy and 1–3 John*, vol. 1 of *Letters and Homilies for Hellenized Christians* (Downers Grove, IL: InterVarsity, 2006), ProQuest Ebook Central, https://ebookcentral.proquest.com/lib/moore/detail .action?docID=2030868), 230–31.

20 See Towner, *Letters*, 143–45.

of full acceptance" (1:15; 4:9). The formula has polemical force and is "a mark of orthodox approval."[21] These sayings are faithful as God is faithful (1 Cor. 1:9; 10:13; 2 Tim. 2:13).[22] In 1 Timothy, each saying speaks to elements of God's salvation plan under threat.

Another distinctive of the letters to Timothy and Titus is the term "sound" (from *hygiainō*) to describe content (1 Tim. 1:10; 6:3; 2 Tim. 1:13; 4:3; Titus 1:9; 2:1; cf. *hygiēs*, Titus 2:8).[23] Elsewhere in the New Testament, the word applies to physical health (e.g., Matt. 12:13; Luke 5:31), but in Timothy and Titus, it refers to *teaching* that is healthy—sound, true, and correct—in sharp contrast to teaching and conduct that are not true and do harm. "Sound" teaching conforms to the gospel (1 Tim. 1:10–11) and produces faith and godly lives (1:4–5).[24] By contrast, false teachers oppose the "healthy/sound" words of Christ and have an unhealthy craving for controversy and depraved (corrupted) minds (6:4–5).[25]

Concluding Observations

The above terms relate to a stable body of content about the appearing of Christ Jesus to save sinners and related doctrine that was recognized as genuine, reliable, authoritative apostolic teaching. A similar notion of fixed content is found across Paul's letters and the New Testament (e.g., Matt. 28:19–20; Gal. 1:6–7; 2 Thess. 2:14–15; 1 John 4:14–15). The various terms draw attention to different aspects of the *one* truth.

It is God's message about God's plan. He is its source, and it reflects his character. It cannot be known apart from divine revelation. The good news of Christ is at its core. It includes theological, missional, ethical, and ecclesial content. It is the standard of truth. Rejection of this message is rejection of God. Its authenticity and preservation are essential for

21 Chiao Ek Ho, "Mission in the Pastoral Epistles," in *EWTG* 250.
22 George W. Knight, *Commentary on the Pastoral Epistles*, NIGTC (Grand Rapids, MI: Eerdmans, 1992), 99.
23 See Robert W. Yarbrough, *The Letters to Timothy and Titus*, PNTC (Grand Rapids, MI: Eerdmans, 2018), 65–67. Cf. "sound in faith" (Titus 1:13; 2:2).
24 Mounce, *Pastoral Epistles*, 42.
25 Knight, *Pastoral Epistles*, 252.

God's saving plan, and the polemical nature of several terms reflects the live threat of false teaching. Paul's apostleship and Timothy's task (and others', 1 Tim. 4:12) are inextricably tied to this content and the command of God and Christ to proclaim, teach, and guard it (1:1; 2:7; 4:16).

God's Word Written

God's written word also features in 1 Timothy, against the backdrop of the false teachers' misuse of the Old Testament. Paul's handling of the Old Testament, through explicit references and allusions, demonstrates both its enduring authority and the need to interpret God's ancient word in light of the gospel (1:11). The letter also testifies to new authoritative content that is coordinate with the Old Testament, namely, Jesus's words as "Scripture" and Paul's letter itself.

The opponents claimed to be experts in the Mosaic law and used the law to support their myths and speculations (1:3–7). Their teaching was wrong, not because of a problem with the law (*nomos*), which is good—and which Paul himself used (see Ex. 20:1–17; Deut. 5:7–21)[26]—but because of their unlawful use of it.[27] Used lawfully (*nominōs*, 1 Tim. 1:8), it was laid down to expose sinners, not "right living" Christians ("the just," 1:9);[28] and it was to be read in its salvation-historical context and in light of the apostolic gospel (1:10–11), not speculative Jewish myths and genealogies.[29]

In fact, Paul turns to the early chapters of Genesis (itself part of the Mosaic Law or Torah) to explain his instructions about proper church leadership, specifically, why women are not to teach or have authority over men (1 Tim. 2:13–14).[30] He cites God's ordered creation of Adam

26 Luke Timothy Johnson, *The First and Second Letters to Timothy*, AB 35A (New York: Doubleday, 2001), 168–69; Marshall, *Pastoral Epistles*, 378–79.

27 See Dillon Thornton, "Sin Seizing the Opportunity through the Commandments," *HBT* 36 (2014): 142–58.

28 Stephen Westerholm, "The Law and the 'Just Man' (1 Tim. 1:3–11)," *ST* 36 (1982): 84.

29 Andreas J. Köstenberger, *Commentary on Timothy and Titus*, BTCP (Nashville: Holman Reference, 2017), 403–5.

30 See Thomas R. Schreiner, "An Interpretation of 1 Timothy 2:9–15: A Dialogue with Scholarship," in *Women in the Church: An Interpretation and Application of 1 Timothy 2:9–15*,

and Eve (Gen. 2:4–25) for the different gendered responsibilities in the church, and he cites the fall narrative, which involved a reversal of their created relational order and a failure of the man's leadership (Gen. 3:13, 17), as a negative example of what happens when God's order is rejected.[31] It is possible that the opponents used these Genesis texts in their *mythical* speculations,[32] but Paul treats them as *historical* accounts, with Adam and Eve also functioning as *representative* figures, such that there are ongoing implications for *Christian* men and women that arise from God's creation design (1 Cor. 11:3–16; 14:33–35; cf. Eph. 5:21–33).[33]

Similarly, when Paul critiques the opponents' ascetic prohibitions against certain foods and marriage, he does so with reference to the early chapters of Genesis. He notes God's generous provision of food (1 Tim. 4:3; cf. Gen. 1:29; 2:9; 9:3)[34] and repeats God's verdict that "everything in creation is good" (1 Tim. 4:4; cf. Gen. 1:31). Genesis also affirms the goodness of marriage (Gen. 1:28; 2:24; cf. 1 Tim. 3:2; 5:14).[35] The opponents, then, were not only rejecting the good gifts of God's creation; they were also rejecting God's word about these gifts and possibly failing to read God's word in light of Christ (see Mark 7:1–23; 10:2–9; Acts 10; Gal. 2:12–14). Paul's view of creation and marriage rests on God's word, which he regards as true, authoritative, and of enduring relevance for Christian believers.

Paul again turns to Scripture to explain his instructions about material support for elders (1 Tim. 5:18). He uses the only citation formula in the letter, "the Scripture [*graphē*] says," to introduce *two* statements: the first, about oxen, from Deuteronomy (Deut. 25:4 LXX); the second, about laborers deserving their wages, from Jesus's words (most likely) from Luke's Gospel (10:7; cf. Matt. 10:10). That is, Jesus's recorded

---

3rd ed., ed. Andreas J. Köstenberger and Thomas R. Schreiner (Wheaton, IL: Crossway, 2016), 199–216.

31 Köstenberger, *Timothy and Titus*, 116–18.

32 Philip H. Towner, "1–2 Timothy and Titus," in *CNTUOT* 896.

33 B. Paul Wolfe, "The Sagacious Use of Scripture," in *EWTG* 204.

34 Towner, "Timothy and Titus," 898.

35 Johnson, *Letters*, 240.

words in that work are identified as divinely inspired Scripture and coordinate with the canonical Old Testament.[36]

Alongside Paul's use of Scripture in the letter, we see the continuing relevance and use of Scripture *in the Christian gathering*, as Paul urges Timothy to devote himself to the public reading of Scripture and its exposition (1 Tim. 4:13). Similar practices in synagogues were based on the Old Testament Scriptures (Acts 13:13–41). We can assume the same here (cf. 2 Cor. 3:14). However, Paul instructs Timothy to teach, exhort, and command the content of his letter (1 Tim. 4:11; 6:2), which was also to be read publicly (6:21),[37] so it's not a stretch to include *this* letter and other apostolic writings as authoritative texts that were also to be the subject of ongoing congregational instruction (Col. 4:16; 1 Thess. 5:27; 2 Thess. 2:15; 2 Peter 3:16; Rev. 1:3).[38]

———

Knowing and believing the truth is essential for salvation (1 Tim. 2:4). That truth is made known in God's word: the apostolic gospel about the Christ event and related apostolic teaching, along with the Old Testament, correctly understood and interpreted through the gospel. It is God's truth: the mystery unable to be known apart from his revelation, explicitly involving each person of the triune God (1:11; 4:1; 5:18 ; 6:3; cf. 1:18; 4:14). Its origin, character, authority, and purpose are given by God. It is a stable and recognized body of content, the saving power of which is evident in the priority given to making it known, and the need to preserve and protect it from deviation or distortion.

Paul's engagement with the Old Testament shows that it is to be read in light of the gospel and God's purposes in salvation history, and that there is continuity and discontinuity between the Old Testament and

---

36 See Michael J. Kruger, "First Timothy 5:18 and Early Canon Consciousness: Reconsidering a Problematic Text," in *The Language and Literature of the New Testament*, ed. Lois K. Fuller Dow, Craig A. Evans, and Andrew W. Pitts (Leiden: Brill, 2017), 680–700.

37 Plural "you" (*hymōn*).

38 Knight, *Pastoral Epistles*, 207–8.

the apostolic message. By contrast, the teachers of the law show that it is possible to *misuse* God's word (1:7). It is not enough to prove something by quoting Scripture; the word must be rightly interpreted and applied. We also see a developing "canon-consciousness," with certain apostolic writings being treated as coordinate sources of divine truth with the Old Testament Scriptures.[39]

---

39 Wolfe, "Sagacious Use," 214; Kruger, "First Timothy 5:18," 694.

4

The Household of God

AT EACH STAGE OF SALVATION HISTORY, God's people are both a means and a goal of his work. He saves a people for himself and dwells with them (Ex. 6:6–7; Rev. 21:3, 7), and his people are to make his name known and advance his purposes in the world (Gen. 12:1–3; 1 Chron. 16:8–36; Col. 1:27). So, too, in 1 Timothy. Dealing with the false teaching was a pressing need (1:3), but Paul also wrote so that Timothy and, through him, the Ephesian Christians would know how to conduct themselves "in the household of God" (3:14–15). In this, despite the particular circumstances for the letter, it has a broader horizon as it addresses the nature and function of the church for all believers in all places and cultures.

God's Grand Plan

One of the key exegetical issues in 1 Timothy is the translation and meaning of the term *oikonomia theou* (1:4). There are three main approaches among Bible translations. One approach follows a textual variant that has the related word "edification" (*oikodomēn*)[1] and focuses on moral exhortation (NKJV; cf. RSV). However, the correct word is almost certainly *oikonomia*, which relates to household management

---

1 See the critical apparatus in *The Greek New Testament*, United Bible Societies, 5th ed.; BDAG, s.v. *oikonomia*, §3.

(*oikos*, "house"/"household" + *nomos*, "law"). A second approach (ESV) understands this as referring to the task of household "stewardship" (see Eph. 3:2; Col. 1:25).[2] And a third approach focuses on the planning, governance, organization, and purpose of the household[3] (CSB, "God's plan"; NET, "God's redemptive plan"; see Eph. 1:10; 3:9).[4] This is my preferred interpretation, but as the implementation of God's plan is indispensable to it, stewardship cannot be excluded.[5]

The gospel is the "theological core"[6] of God's *oikonomia*, but its scope is broader than salvation. It is a divinely organized pattern or plan of all things, where no aspect of creation or human life or society is exempted, and where everything has its proper God-given place and role to play and is to be directed toward his desire that all people would be saved (1 Tim. 2:4); and it extends to the pattern or order of life that is to be embraced, obeyed, and defended by those in God's household, which occupies much of the letter.[7] It is "God's way of ordering things,"[8] his "household rules,"[9] "God's grand, eternal plan to consummate all things in Christ."[10]

This eternal divine plan is perceived and responded to *by faith* (*en pistei*, 1:4) in what God has revealed in Scripture and history.[11] Sin opposes, rejects, and misaligns with what God is doing and has revealed concerning his way of ordering the world—for example, in the Law (1:8; 5:18–19), in creation (2:13–14; 4:3–5), and, chiefly, in the apos-

---

2   So, I. Howard Marshall, *The Pastoral Epistles*, ICC (Edinburgh: T&T Clark, 1999), 367.

3   LSJ, s.v. *oikonomia*.

4   ESV footnote, "good order."

5   Gerald L. Bray, *The Pastoral Epistles*, ITC (London: T&T Clark, 2019), 89–90.

6   Greg A. Couser, "The Sovereign Savior of 1 and 2 Timothy and Titus," in *EWTG* 112.

7   See Couser, "Sovereign Savior," 112–16. Philip H. Towner, *The Letters to Timothy and Titus*, NICNT (Grand Rapids, MI: Eerdmans, 2006), 68–70.

8   Luke Timothy Johnson, *The First and Second Letters to Timothy*, AB 35A (New York: Doubleday, 2001), 149; followed by Towner, *Letters*, 69, 113; Abraham Kuruvilla, *1 & 2 Timothy, Titus: A Theological Commentary for Preachers* (Eugene, OR: Cascade, 2021), 21.

9   Couser, "Sovereign Savior," 112.

10 Kuruvilla, *Timothy, Titus*, 22.

11 Robert W. Yarbrough, *The Letters to Timothy and Titus*, PNTC (Grand Rapids, MI: Eerdmans, 2018), 105.

tolic gospel (1:10–11).[12] Paul sinned like this, but he received mercy and grace from Christ (1:13–16). This is the error of the opponents, whose myths and genealogies promote speculation, not faith in Christ (1:3–7). But they, too, are not beyond hope (1:16, 20; 5:20).

The Household of the Living God

The *oikonomia theou* is the grand plan of God for all eternity; "the household of God" is the realization of that plan in history; and Paul writes so that believers will know how to conduct themselves in that household (3:14–15).

Paul often uses metaphors for the Christian community (e.g., human "body," "temple," "bride"). The main metaphor in 1 Timothy is the "house" or "household of God" (*oikos theou*, 3:15; cf. Eph. 2:19; 2 Tim. 2:20; Titus 1:7).[13] Some interpreters consider this a reference to Christian believers as the new temple of God (see Heb. 3:6; 1 Pet. 2:5; cf. *naos*, 1 Cor. 3:16; Eph. 2:21).[14] Although the architectural terms in 1 Timothy 3:15 lend support to that view, the dominant motif is that of the household, as this theologically rich term is linguistically and conceptually related to God's *oikonomia* and is further developed in the correspondence between individual families and the church (3:4–5, 12; 5:1–2, 4). Paul uses similar images elsewhere (1 Cor. 3:9; 4:1–2; 9:17; Gal. 6:10; Col. 1:25).

Paul does not use this metaphor to impose the social hierarchies and values of Greco-Roman households onto the church.[15] Rather,

---

12 George M. Wieland, "Re-Ordering the Household: Misalignment and Realignment to God's *oikonomia* in 1 Timothy," in *Sin and Its Remedy in Paul*, ed. Nijay Gupta and John K. Goodrich, Contours of Pauline Theology (Eugene, OR: Cascade, 2020), 159.

13 Johnson, *Letters*, 231; George W. Knight, *Commentary on the Pastoral Epistles*, NIGTC (Grand Rapids, MI: Eerdmans, 1992), 180; Andreas J. Köstenberger, *Commentary on 1–2 Timothy and Titus*, BTCP (Nashville: Holman Reference, 2017), 450.

14 So, William D. Mounce, *Pastoral Epistles*, WBC 46 (Nashville: Thomas Nelson, 2000), 220–21.

15 For example, as claimed by David C. Verner, *The Household of God: The Social World of the Pastoral Epistles* (Chico, CA: Scholars Press, 1983), 160, 182, 186; Francis Young, *The Theology of the Pastoral Letters*, New Testament Theology (Cambridge: Cambridge University Press, 1994), 121.

aspects of Greco-Roman and Jewish households map onto God's household by way of illustration. For example, God occupies the central role and authority of the household head, the *paterfamilias*, (not human fathers or leaders), and members receive identity, refuge, protection, and provision from him; there is an expectation of unity and conformity to the master's will, and there are notions of stewardship and belonging, recognized standards of conduct, and mutual responsibilities and loyalty of members.[16] The household is also where children are educated.[17]

Salvation-historically, God's household—like his temple—is where God dwells with his people (Gen. 28:17; Ex. 23:19; 2 Sam. 7). It is the fulfillment of his Old Testament promises and purpose to create a people for his own possession and dwell among them (e.g., Deut. 7:6; 2 Cor. 6:16; Rev. 22:3–4). As God's household, the church is to be "the microcosm or paradigm of a world obedient to God's ordering; and its mission is to extend this reality beyond its walls."[18]

The local gathering of believers is also a "church [*ekklēsia*] of the living God" (1 Tim. 3:15; cf. 1 Cor. 1:2; 2 Cor. 1:1; 1 Tim. 3:5; 5:16).[19] He is a "living" and active presence with them. In the Old Testament, the redeemed people of God were assembled by God to hear his word, learn his ways, and respond in worship (LXX: Deut. 4:10; 18:16).[20] The same activities are to characterize his new assemblies (e.g., 1 Tim. 2:1, 8; 4:5, 13).

The church is "a pillar and foundation of the truth" (3:15 YLT; cf. Gen. 28:12–22). "The truth" is the full body of revealed orthodox content, centered on the gospel and including doctrine and ethics. Knowledge of the truth is necessary for salvation (1 Tim. 2:4). The church,

---

16 Philip H. Towner, "Households and Household Codes," in *DPL* 417–18; Köstenberger, *Timothy and Titus*, 452.

17 See Margaret Y. MacDonald, "Education and the Household in the Pastoral Epistles," *Int* 75, no. 4 (2021): 283–93.

18 Towner, *Letters*, 69.

19 Benjamin L. Merkle, "Ecclesiology in the Pastoral Epistles," in *EWTG* 174; Mounce, *Pastoral Epistles*, 220, 222.

20 Peter T. O'Brien, "Church," in *DPL* 124.

especially its leadership, is to pray for and advance the proclamation of the truth (2:1–3; 3:16), defend it from attacks (1:3; 6:20),[21] and bear testimony to truth through its presence in the world (3:7; 5:8; 6:1).[22]

The Christian community in first-century Ephesus, and in every other place (2:8) and period of history, is the "household *of God*" and assembly "*of the living God.*" His ownership and presence provide the urgency and force of Paul's instructions and ethical demands, and underscore the gravity of the opponents' activities. The opponents were harming the people and dwelling place of *God*, not a mere human institution.

Life in God's Household

God's household comprises those who are saved, both Jews and Gentiles (1:2; 2:7). Membership is not static. God adds people to his household, but each one must take care to remain in salvation (2:15; 4:16; 6:11–12). Some, like Hymenaeus and Alexander, appeared at one time to belong but put themselves outside God's *spiritual* household. For their sake, Paul delivered them over to Satan for educative discipline by expelling them from the church in the hope that they would repent (1:19–20; cf. Matt. 18:15–20; 1 Cor. 5:5).[23]

Members of God's household are bound to one another in familial allegiance of duty, love, and service. Irrespective of age or station in life, they are beloved brothers and sisters (1 Tim. 4:6; cf. Mark 3:31–35)— even slaves with their masters (1 Tim. 6:2)—who equally know God as Father (1:2; cf. Gal. 3:26).[24] However, these familial bonds don't negate God-given order and obligations in the family and church. Fathers are to provide leadership and spiritual instruction (1 Tim. 3:4; cf. Deut. 6:4–9); children are to submit to their fathers (1 Tim. 3:4; cf. Ex. 20:12; Eph. 6:1–4; Col. 3:20); family members are to provide for widows

21 Marshall, *Pastoral Epistles*, 423; Kuruvilla, *Timothy, Titus*, 78.

22 Köstenberger, *Timothy and Titus*, 466.

23 Dillon T. Thornton, *Hostility in the House of God: An Investigation of the Opponents in 1 and 2 Timothy*, BBRSup 15 (Winona Lake, IN: Eisenbrauns, 2016), 51–55.

24 See Gregory J. Stiekes, "Paul's Family of God: What Familial Language in the Pastorals Can and Cannot Tell Us about the Church," *STR* 7, no. 2 (2016): 35–56.

(1 Tim. 5:4, 8, 16; cf. Deut. 27:16; Job 29:12–17; Ps. 68:5–6); and wives and mothers are to fulfill their family responsibilities (1 Tim. 2:10, 15; 5:10, 14; cf. Gen. 1:28; Prov. 31).

Unexpectedly for modern readers, Christian slaves[25] must render due honor and service to their masters, all the more so if they too are believers (1 Tim. 6:1–2; cf. Eph. 6:5–9; Col. 3:22–4:1; Titus 2:9–10; 1 Pet. 2:18). Paul is *not* here endorsing the institution of slavery, even less the exploitation, injustice, abuse, and racism we associate with it. His instructions have a missional intention, because failure to follow them would have caused evil to be spoken (*blasphemeō*) of God's name and the gospel.[26] Slavery was widespread in antiquity,[27] but the only slavery about which the New Testament speaks positively is believers' slavery to Christ in obedience (Rom. 6:22; 1 Cor. 7:23; Titus 1:1; 1 Pet. 2:16). Otherwise, Paul urges slaves who can to gain their freedom (1 Cor. 7:21). Importantly, he always addresses slaves as full members of the church and moral agents equal to their masters. Here, they are even their masters' benefactors (1 Tim. 6:2).[28] That is, through the familial bonds of faith and love, Paul is turning the conventional social order on its head, even while upholding it!

Relationships in God's household are analogous to those he established within families: there are sibling bonds of faith (4:6; 6:2); Timothy is Paul's "true child" (1:2, 18; cf. 1 Cor. 4:17; 2 Tim. 3:10);[29] Timothy is to exhort church members as he would the equivalent family member (1 Tim. 5:1–2); the church is to provide for widows without families to care for them (5:3, 9, 16); men are assigned teaching and governing responsibilities in the church (2:11–12; 3:1–7; cf. 1 Cor. 14:33–35), reflecting the ordered complementarity of God's design for marriage (1 Tim. 2:13–14; cf. Gen. 2:18, 23–24; Eph. 5:22–33; Col. 3:18–19; Titus 2:5; 1 Pet. 3:1–7); and the role of overseer/elder

25 ESV footnote, "bondservants."
26 Knight, *Pastoral Epistles*, 246.
27 See A. A. Rupprecht, "Slavery," in *DPL* 881–83.
28 Towner, *Letters*, 386.
29 MacDonald, "Education," 285.

corresponds to managing one's home (1 Tim. 3:4–5; 5:17),[30] including in the role of teacher.[31]

Paul expects the church to comprise a network of households.[32] Marriage is good (4:3; cf. 3:2; 5:9). Family is good (2:15; 5:10, 14). Both are primary spheres for godliness (*"first* learn," 5:4; cf. 3:4, 12; 5:8, 14, 16). Conduct in the home impacts membership and ministry in God's household,[33] for good (3:2–5, 11–12; 5:9–10) and for ill (1:9; 5:8, 11–16), and failure to fulfill family obligations damages the church's mission (3:7; 5:8, 14).[34]

Order in God's Household

The remedy and future of the church in Ephesus rests on sound church leadership. So, in Paul's absence, in addition to silencing opponents and actively teaching truth, Timothy is given instructions for ensuring godly, gifted, and orderly leadership of God's household (3:14–15).

Overseer/Elder

In the letters to Timothy and Titus, "overseer" (*episkopos*, 3:1–2; Titus 1:7; cf. Phil. 1:1) and "elder" (*presbyteros*, 1 Tim. 5:17, 19; Titus 1:5; cf. 1 Pet. 5:1) refer to the same office and function (cf. Acts 20:17, 28).[35] Both terms are associated with supervisory responsibilities and seniority.[36] There is a plurality of overseers/elders, with leadership, management (*proistēmi*, 1 Tim. 3:4, 5; 5:17), and teaching responsibilities (3:2; 5:17),[37] although it's likely that not all shared equally in

30 Towner, *Letters*, 254–55.
31 MacDonald, "Education," 290.
32 John M. G. Barclay, "Household Networks and Early Christian Economics: A Fresh Study of 1 Timothy 5:3–16," *NTS* 66 (2020): 275.
33 See Charles J. Bumgardner, "Kinship, Christian Kinship, and the Letters to Timothy and Titus," *STR* 7, no. 2 (2016): 3–17.
34 Chiao Ek Ho, "Mission in the Pastoral Epistles," in *EWTG* 252–53.
35 See Merkle, "Ecclesiology," 180–90.
36 Towner, *Letters*, 245–47.
37 Gordon D. Fee, *1 and 2 Timothy, Titus*, NIBC (Peabody, MA: Hendrickson, 1988), 22; Philip H. Towner, *The Goal of Our Instruction: The Structure of Theology and Ethics in the Pastoral Epistles*, JSNTSup 34 (Sheffield: JSOT, 1989), 223–27.

teaching.[38] Together they constituted a council of elders (4:14),[39] which was a subset of all older men (5:1).

The office of overseer is a "noble task" (3:1), but it is not open to everyone. First, men who do not meet the selection criteria are excluded. And, second, women are not eligible—not because they were, at the time, uneducated or influenced by false teaching or lacked gifts, or because of patriarchal social mores—but because God's creation design of ordered complementarity between the sexes assigns leadership in God's household to men. Hence, in *his* household, in first-century Ephesus and in all places and cultures, women are to learn quietly and not teach (*didaskein*) or have authority over (*authentein*) men (2:11–14; cf. 1 Cor. 14:33–35), which are the key tasks of overseers.[40]

Beyond that, the selection criteria prioritize the reputations of the men and the church,[41] and require demonstrated ability in the two key responsibilities of the role, namely, teaching of sound doctrine (1 Tim. 3:2) and managing their own households as they would God's own (3:4–5; cf. Titus 1:6–9). Overseers are to exemplify the virtues demanded of all believers (Heb. 13:7; 1 Pet. 5:3).[42] They must be mature believers (1 Tim. 3:6) with no serious flaws that would bring reproach, scandal, or dishonor (3:2, 7, 10, 13). There is a high bar set for their conduct, and their discipline if they persist in sin (5:19–20). The ultimate concern is that God's saving plan is advanced.

They were appointed with laying on of hands, Timothy's and maybe others'[43] (5:22; cf. Acts 14:23), but implicitly, as it is God's household, it is God who decides. The critical place of teaching in God's household

---

38 Köstenberger, *Timothy and Titus*, 126; Fee, *Timothy, Titus*, 128; Donald Guthrie, *The Pastoral Epistles*, TNTC (1957; repr., Leicester: Inter-Varsity Press, 1984), 105.

39 Johnson, *Letters*, 253.

40 See Thomas R. Schreiner, "An Interpretation of 1 Timothy 2:9–15: A Dialogue with Scholarship," in *Women in the Church: An Interpretation and Application of 1 Timothy 2:9–15*, 3rd ed., ed. Andreas J. Köstenberger and Thomas R. Schreiner (Wheaton, IL: Crossway, 2016), 199–216; Andreas J. Köstenberger, "Hermeneutical and Exegetical Challenges in Interpreting the Pastoral Epistles," in *EWTG* 17–22.

41 Towner, *Goal*, 232.

42 Kuruvilla, *Timothy, Titus*, 68.

43 Knight, *Pastoral Epistles*, 239; Towner, *Letters*, 374.

(1 Tim. 1:19; 2:4; 3:15) is reflected in the double material honor[44] due to those who labor in preaching and teaching (5:17).[45]

Deacons: Male and Female

The eligibility criteria for deacons (*diakonos*, 3:8, 12; cf. Rom. 16:1; Phil. 1:1) relate to the second tier of church leadership. The qualifications resemble those for overseers in regard to virtuous conduct and blameless reputation. As with overseers, the list is representative rather than exhaustive,[46] and there is blessing and honor in the task (1 Tim. 3:1, 13).[47] The ability to teach is not listed. Evidently, responsibility for authoritative teaching was the task of overseers. Deacons likely complemented their ministry, serving in other aspects of congregational life and care.[48] A similar division of labor is seen early in the Jerusalem church (Acts 6:1–6). Here in Ephesus, as there, candidates are chosen for their faith in Christ, sound doctrine, and godly life (1 Tim. 3:9–10).

Some interpreters and Bible translations understand 3:11 to refer to wives generally, or the wives of deacons[49] or of deacons and overseers.[50] The Greek word (*gynaikas*) will allow all these; however, the context favors female deacons.[51] Additionally, the teaching and governing roles that preclude women from being overseers are not mentioned for deacons, and the term is used elsewhere for a woman serving the church (see Rom. 16:1 ESV footnote). Either way, we see women, like their male counterparts, involved in recognized ministry roles, with high eligibility criteria and standing in the church community.

---

44 Johnson, *Letters*, 277.
45 Marshall, *Pastoral Epistles*, 612; Knight, *Pastoral Epistles*, 232; Merkle, "Ecclesiology," 189–90.
46 Yarbrough, *Letters*, 190.
47 Kuruvilla, *Timothy, Titus*, 75.
48 Merkle, "Ecclesiology," 191.
49 ESV main text.
50 See Yarbrough, *Letters*, 209–11.
51 See Köstenberger, *Timothy and Titus*, 131–35; Bray, *Pastoral Epistles*, 194–95.

Widows

Enrolled widows (*chēra*) were to have a reputation for good works and had "recognised standing" in the church,[52] but probably did not have a formal ministry role or order (1 Tim. 5:9–12).[53]

Timothy

Timothy's ministry in Ephesus was an apostolic response to the needs there. He was not an overseer or deacon, and his authority was not like theirs. The Ephesian church did not appoint him. He was a visiting apostolic delegate—authorized and directed by Paul—whose special gifting from God and ministry were indicated through prophecies and recognized through the laying on of hands (1:18; 4:14; cf. 2 Tim. 1:6; Acts 13:2–3). Yet Timothy himself was to appoint and rebuke elders (1 Tim. 5:19–22).[54] His ministry effectively overrode conventional social relations as his youth posed no obstacle to his leadership and authority, even over elders; and he was able to provide an example of belief and life to *all* believers (4:12; cf. 1 Cor. 4:17; 16:10–11).[55]

Timothy is described as a "servant [*diakonos*] of Christ Jesus" (1 Tim. 4:6) and "man of God" (6:11)[56] not in a recognized office.[57] But he was to display the necessary qualities for good leadership par excellence, in sharp contrast to the opponents. He was to flee their myths and way of life and "pursue righteousness, godliness, faith, love, steadfastness, gentleness" (6:4–11), set an example "in speech, in conduct, in love, in faith, in purity," and devote himself to the public ministry of God's word (4:1–7, 11–16).

The vision of the church as the household of the living God is theologically and missiologically driven, and has at its heart the salvation plan

52 Bray, *Pastoral Epistles*, 252.
53 Johnson, *Letters*, 271.
54 Merkle, "Ecclesiology," 196–97.
55 See David W. Pao, "Let No One Despise Your Youth: Church and the World in the Pastoral Epistles," *JETS* 57 (2014): 743–55.
56 Yarbrough, *Letters*, 321, notes use of this term in the LXX.
57 Towner, *Goal*, 229. "Evangelist" in 2 Tim. 4:5 might be a recognized role.

of God, who wants all types of people to be saved. God's household is formed by, ordered for, and primarily directed toward the gospel—not first-century cultural norms—and conveys the rich privileges and duties of belonging as his children, and notions of delegated responsibility, education, order, and obedience.

Until Christ's appearing, believers are to conform to God's ordering in their own lives and households; and as *God's* household, they and especially their leaders are to work toward the same goal, both in the church's internal life and in its engagement with the surrounding society and the public square. As Philip Towner observes, "Ultimately, beyond simply facilitating the self-maintenance of the community, this 'household' order serves the Church in its role as the 'supporting foundation of the truth' in which role it has interface with the world."[58]

---

58 Towner, *Goal*, 143.

5

The Promise of Godliness

PAUL IS INSISTENT THAT TIMOTHY and the Ephesians know how they are to live godly lives as the household of God (1 Tim. 3:15). But the promise of godliness is not only for this life. It has an eschatological horizon (4:8), such that the present life of faith cannot be understood apart from eternal life. Both are defined and located within God's time-table, established by the past and future appearings of Christ. Christ himself is the "mystery of godliness" now revealed (3:16; cf. 3:9). Ethics and eschatology belong together.

Godliness Manifest in Love

The goal of Paul's instruction in this letter—and his apostleship, and all genuine Christian existence and ministry, including Timothy's need to prevent false teaching—is love (1:5). The false teachers had seared consciences and depraved minds, and were devoid of the truth (1:19; 4:2; 6:5), and their teaching promoted speculation, discord, and distrust, not God's ordering of all things (1:4; 6:3–5). Their teaching on the law couldn't change morally corrupt sinners (1:9–10).[1] Only Christ can do that, as Paul's experience demonstrates (1:13, 16; cf. Rom. 8:3–4). This is the power of the apostolic gospel, which, by contrast, produces godly

---

1 Luke Timothy Johnson, *The First and Second Letters to Timothy*, AB 35A (New York: Doubleday, 2001), 153.

lives of love that promote and accord with God's plan, and come from "a pure heart, a good conscience, and a sincere faith." There are only two ways to live; and there is a clear correlation between the content of *belief* and the kind of *life* it produces, and also between the inner person and the outward life.

Genuine faith produces love of God and neighbor (Deut. 6:4–5; Matt. 22:34–40).[2] Love is "the zenith of godliness" and greatest of the commandments.[3] Every occurrence of "love" (*agapē*) in the letters to Timothy and Titus, bar one (2 Tim. 1:7), is paired with "faith" (1 Tim. 1:5, 14; 2:15; 4:12; 6:11; 2 Tim. 1:13; 2:22; 3:10; Titus 2:2).[4] God's plan operates by faith and manifests in self-giving love—seen supremely in Christ's sacrificial self-giving (1 Tim. 2:6; cf. John 13:34)—and in "good works"[5] (1 Tim. 2:10; 5:10, 25; 6:18; cf. Eph. 2:10; 1 Tim. 3:1; 2 Tim. 2:21; 3:17; Titus 1:16; 2:7; 3:1, 8, 14). Faith is the invisible posture of belief in Christ; love and good works are faith's visible outworking in the Christian life.[6]

As in Paul's other letters, the contours of godliness are developed by way of contrast with attitudes and conduct that do not accord with the gospel (1 Tim. 1:11). There are virtue lists (3:2–4; 4:12; 6:11; cf. Gal. 5:22–23; 2 Tim. 2:22; 3:10) and vice lists (1 Tim. 1:9–10; 6:3–5; cf. Gal. 5:19–21; 2 Tim. 3:2–5; Titus 3:3),[7] as well as negative examples to avoid (Eve, pre-Christian Paul, opponents, neglectful family, some widows, the selfish, the rich) and positive models to emulate (Paul: 1 Tim. 1:2, 15–16; cf. 2 Tim. 3:10; Timothy: 1 Tim. 4:12; cf. Titus 2:7;

2   Jerome D. Quinn and W. C. Wacker, *The First and Second Letters to Timothy: A New Translation with Notes and Commentary*, ECC (Grand Rapids, MI: Eerdmans, 2000), 78–79.

3   Abraham Kuruvilla, *1 & 2 Timothy, Titus: A Theological Commentary for Preachers* (Eugene, OR: Cascade, 2021), 22.

4   William D. Mounce, *Pastoral Epistles*, WBC 46 (Nashville: Thomas Nelson, 2000), 23.

5   See Philip H. Towner, *The Letters to Timothy and Titus*, NICNT (Grand Rapids, MI: Eerdmans, 2006), 210–12.

6   Dillon T. Thornton, *Hostility in the House of God: An Investigation of the Opponents in 1 and 2 Timothy*, BBRSup 15 (Winona Lake, IN: Eisenbrauns, 2016), 41.

7   See Andreas J. Köstenberger, *Commentary on 1–2 Timothy and Titus*, BTCP (Nashville: Holman Reference, 2017), 484–88.

Christ Jesus: 1 Tim. 6:13[8]). Many of the ethical terms are found in Paul's other letters, although some are limited to 1 and 2 Timothy and Titus or other parts of the New Testament. Some interpreters see these terms as a concession to Hellenistic values and a diminution of Pauline ethics.[9] However, while the literary *form* of the ethical material and some *terms* seem to have been taken over from secular culture, the *content* has been reclaimed for Christian use and rests firmly on the Old Testament and the apostolic gospel.[10] It may be that Paul was counteracting the opponents' use of the same material.[11] Whatever the case, it fits well with the letter's missional approach, where believers are not to withdraw from society but to be present in it in culturally meaningful but distinctively Christian ways (1 Tim. 2:1–2; 3:7; cf. 1 Pet. 3:14–16).[12]

One such ethical term is "godliness" (*eusebeia*, 1 Tim. 2:2; 3:16; 4:7–8; 6:3, 5–6, 11; *eusebeō*, 5:4; cf. Acts 3:12; 10:2, 7; 2 Tim. 3:5, 12; Titus 1:1; 2:12). It is frequently found in Greek ethical texts, but its meaning in 1 and 2 Timothy and Titus is redefined and reoriented by the Christ event (1 Tim. 3:16; cf. 2 Tim. 3:12; Titus 2:12).[13] "Godliness" describes the new life possible only for believers in Christ: the belief, character, and conduct that come from saving knowledge of the truth. This reflects the use of the terminology in Hellenistic Judaism for the knowledge and "fear of the Lord," and the response and conduct that flow from them in covenant loyalty (LXX: Prov. 1:7; Isa. 11:2; 33:6).[14]

8   Johnson, *Letters*, 313.
9   For example, Martin Dibelius and Hans Conzelmann, *The Pastoral Epistles*, trans. Philip Buttolph and Adela Yarbro, Hermeneia (Philadelphia: Fortress, 1972), 39–41; Raymond F. Collins, *1 and 2 Timothy, Titus: A Commentary*, New Testament Library (Louisville: Westminster John Knox, 2002), 126.
10 Köstenberger, *Timothy, Titus*, 487; Philip H. Towner, *The Goal of Our Instruction: The Structure of Theology and Ethics in the Pastoral Epistles*, JSNTSup 34 (Sheffield: JSOT, 1989), 160.
11 So, Gordon D. Fee, *1 and 2 Timothy, Titus*, NIBC (Peabody, MA: Hendrickson, 1988), 63.
12 See Towner, *Goal*, 160–65, 250–54.
13 For the history of interpretation of *eusebeia* in the letters to Timothy and Titus, see I. Howard Marshall, *The Pastoral Epistles*, ICC (Edinburgh: T&T Clark, 1999), 135–44; Robert W. Yarbrough, *The Letters to Timothy and Titus*, PNTC (Grand Rapids, MI: Eerdmans, 2018), 62–63.
14 Towner, *Letters*, 173.

And, as with the Old Testament concept of the "fear of the Lord," the godly life in the letters to Timothy and Titus is likewise holistic. It encompasses believers' faith-based relationship with God, their inner person, and their relationship with the created world, the family, the church, and wider society.

Relationship with God

Faith is necessary for salvation and is the ongoing response of those who are saved (1 Tim. 1:5, 14, 16, 19; 2:15; 4:12). Faith is expressed by relating rightly to God and living rightly before him (2:3; 5:4, 21; 6:13; cf. 2 Tim. 2:14–15; 4:1) in hope and dependence (1 Tim. 1:1; 4:10; 5:5; 6:8, 17), prayer and thanksgiving (2:1, 8; 4:3–5), and obedience (1:8–11; 4:5; 5:18), and by engaging rightly with his creation and not being enslaved to it (3:3, 8; 4:3–5, 8; 5:23), and by sharing his desire that all may be saved (1:11–12; 2:1; 4:6, 16; 6:20).

New Life in Christ

The new life of love (1:5) issues from "a pure heart" cleansed of sin (2 Tim. 2:22; Ps. 50:1–12 LXX), a "good conscience" (*syneidēsis*) cleared of guilt and able rightly to discern moral demands (1 Tim. 1:19; 3:9; 4:2; cf. 2 Tim. 1:3), and an undivided faith cultivated in the truth (1 Tim. 4:2).[15] It is not mere outer performance but visible evidence of inner transformation brought about by grace (1:14).[16] At the same time, believers are to devote themselves to developing godly character and lives. Timothy is to fight and flee the opponents' evil *conduct* (1:6, 19; 6:3–5, 11), as well as their teaching; pursue and train himself in *godliness*, as well as teach the truth;[17] and present himself as a model of godly living for all believers to emulate (1:18–19; 4:6–7, 12; 6:11; cf. 2 Tim. 2:22).

Authentic Christian existence involves being *and* doing. There are new personal qualities of "righteousness, godliness, faith, love, stead-

---

15 Gerald L. Bray, *The Pastoral Epistles*, ITC (London: T&T Clark, 2019), 92–94; Kuruvilla, *Timothy, Titus*, 22.

16 Fee, *Timothy, Titus*, 52.

17 Towner, *Letters*, 140–41.

fastness, gentleness"[18] (1 Tim. 6:11; cf. 3:3); self-control (*sōphrosynē*, 2:9, 15; 3:2; cf. 2 Tim. 1:7; Titus 1:8; 2:2, 4–6, 12);[19] modesty (1 Tim. 2:9);[20] humility (3:6; 6:2–5); contentment (6:6–8); purity, perhaps especially sexual purity (4:12; 5:2, 22);[21] and new priorities: cherishing the reputation of the church over personal ambition (3:6), godly character over physical appearance (2:9–10; cf. Prov. 31:30), and eternal treasure over earthly treasure (1 Tim. 6:17–19; cf. 3:3, 8).

These inner qualities manifest themselves in peaceful, quiet (*hēsychios*, 2:2; *hēsychia*, 2:11–12; cf. 1 Thess. 4:11), and godly, dignified lives (1 Tim. 2:2; 3:4, 8, 11; cf. Titus 2:2, 7).[22] Such lives are characterized by

- love (1 Tim. 1:5; 2:15; 6:2);
- speech, without lies, anger or self-seeking (1:10; 2:8; 3:3, 8; 4:12; 5:13; 6:4);
- right use of the body and created things (1:10; 3:3, 8; 4:3–5, 8;[23] 5:23);
- conduct that accords with sex, age, and life-station,[24] whether among men and women (2:8–15; 5:14); fathers,[25] mothers, and children (1:9; 3:4, 12; 5:4–16; cf. Titus 2:4); elders and church members (1 Tim. 3:5; 5:17–21); apostle and delegate (1:2, 12, 18; 3:14–15; 4:13); citizens toward rulers (2:1–2; cf. Titus 3:1); or slaves toward masters (1 Tim. 1:10; 6:1–2; cf. Titus 2:9);
- marital faithfulness (1 Tim. 1:10; 3:2, 12; 5:9; cf. Heb. 13:4);
- hospitality (1 Tim. 3:2; 5:10; cf. Titus 1:8);
- generosity (1 Tim. 6:18);
- respect (4:12; 5:1–3).

18 Marshall, *Pastoral Epistles*, 657.
19 See Marshall, *Pastoral Epistles*, 182–84.
20 Marshall, *Pastoral Epistles*, 448.
21 Bray, *Pastoral Epistles*, 231, 245, 268.
22 Towner, *Letters*, 174–5.
23 See George W. Knight, *Commentary on the Pastoral Epistles*, NIGTC (Grand Rapids, MI: Eerdmans, 1992), 195–99.
24 Greg A. Couser, "The Sovereign Savior of 1 and 2 Timothy and Titus," in *EWTG* 121.
25 See Yarbrough, *Letters*, 199–201.

In short, the godly life is one with character, attitudes, thoughts, speech, and conduct that are aligned with God's ordering of the world and his mission to save. Such a life promotes and commends his salvation to the watching world (2:1–3; 3:7; 5:14; 6:1).[26]

The Present Life

Godliness holds promise for this age and the age to come (4:8). God is the King of the ages (*aiōnōn*) and alone has immortality (1:17; 6:16). All time is under his rule. He established his plan of salvation and, according to his own perfect timing (*kairois idiois*, 2:6; 6:15; cf. Titus 1:3), has revealed and accomplished this "mystery" in the Christ event (1 Tim. 3:9, 16; cf. Col. 1:27).[27] The nature and timing of the two temporal horizons of Christian existence, then, are *Christologically* determined. This "present age" (*nyn aiōn*, 1 Tim. 6:17; cf. 2 Tim. 4:10; Titus 2:12) is the epoch between Christ's first (1 Tim. 3:16; cf. Titus 2:11; 3:4) and second appearings (1 Tim. 6:14; cf. 2 Tim. 4:1, 8; Titus 2:13) in history: the inauguration and in-breaking of God's redemptive plan, and its final future consummation. Both decisively reset the conditions, possibilities, and imperatives of life.[28] It means that "now" is the time of salvation (cf. 2 Cor. 6:2). The anticipated inclusion of the nations in God's salvation plan has arrived (1 Tim. 2:1–7; 3:16; cf. Isa. 2:2–3; Mic. 4:1–2; Matt. 28:19),[29] and so have the increasing spiritual opposition, apostasy, and false teaching of these "later times" (*hysterois kairois*, 1 Tim. 4:1; cf. Gal. 1:4; 2 Tim. 3:1) against God's people and mission.[30] *Salvation history*, not human history, determines the meaning and nature of the times.

Believers are saved and receive eternal life in this present age (1 Tim. 1:15–16; 6:12; cf. Rom. 6:4), but full realization of that life is in the age

---

26 Couser, "Sovereign Savior," 120.

27 G. K. Beale and Benjamin L. Gladd, *Hidden but Now Revealed: A Biblical Theology of Mystery* (Downers Grove, IL: InterVarsity Press, 2014), 237–59.

28 Towner, *Goal*, 69.

29 Andreas J. Köstenberger, "Mission," in *NDBT* 664.

30 Gregory K. Beale, *A New Testament Biblical Theology: The Unfolding of the Old Testament in the New* (Grand Rapids, MI: Baker Academic, 2011), 141, 820–21; Fee, *Timothy, Titus*, 98.

to come.[31] In the meantime, they share in "the eschatological age here and now in anticipation of life in the eschaton."[32] This is not a guarantee of health (1 Tim. 5:23) or wealth (6:6–10, 17–19) or trouble-free existence (5:5, 11; 6:1, 13; cf. 2 Tim. 3:10–12) in this world. It is the spiritual blessing of sharing in the life of the life-giving, immortal, living God (1 Tim. 1:17; 4:10; 6:13, 16), such that "the life of God activates, animates or is mirrored by those who profess faith in him."[33]

This *is* "truly life" (6:19; cf. John 10:10),[34] but it's a mixed already-and-not-yet experience, where contentment with simple provisions is virtuous (1 Tim. 6:6–8, 17),[35] and self-sacrificial toil and struggle (4:10; 6:12; cf. 2 Tim. 4:7),[36] perseverance (1 Tim. 6:11), faith, and hope are still needed.[37] Those who live for self and not for God are even now spiritually "dead" (5:6; cf. Eph. 2:1).[38] They deny the way of Christ (1 Tim. 2:6).

The Life to Come

The present age, and Christian existence therein, lasts "until" the second appearing of our Lord Jesus Christ (6:14), which marks the transition to the age to come (4:8; 6:19). Some interpreters claim that active expectation of Christ's imminent return has been replaced in the letters to Timothy and Titus by disappointed hope and the desire for mere peaceful coexistence with the world.[39] But Paul elsewhere encourages believers to live peaceably with this world (Rom. 13:1–7; 1 Thess. 4:11),

---

31 Ben Witherington III, *A Socio-Rhetorical Commentary on Titus, 1–2 Timothy and 1–3 John*, vol. 1 of *Letters and Homilies for Hellenized Christians* (Downers Grove, IL: InterVarsity, 2006), ProQuest Ebook Central, https://ebookcentral.proquest.com/lib/moore/detail.action?docID=2030868), 208.

32 Mounce, *Pastoral Epistles*, 59.

33 Aldred A. Genade, "Life in the Pauline Letters (3): Life in the Pastoral Epistles," in *Biblical Theology of Life in the New Testament*, ed. F. P. Viljoen and A. J. Coetsee (Cape Town: AOSIS, 2021), 122.

34 Yarbrough, *Letters*, 338.

35 Mounce, *Pastoral Epistles*, 337–38.

36 Yarbrough, Letters, 324.

37 See Towner, *Goal*, 152.

38 Kuruvilla, *Timothy, Titus*, 105–6.

39 So, classically, Dibelius and Conzelmann, *Pastoral Epistles*, 9–10.

and despite some different terminology, there *is* expectation of Christ's return in Paul's letters to his delegates (1 Tim. 6:14; 2 Tim. 1:12, 18; 4:1, 8; Titus 2:13). So, while the letters focus on Christian existence in the present age, they do so *in the context of Christ's return and the age to come*. In 1 Timothy, this eschatological perspective has at least four dimensions.

The first is *theological*. Christ Jesus is "our hope" (1:1; cf. Titus 2:13; Col. 1:27), and God our Savior is the object of believers' hope for the present life and the life to come (1 Tim. 4:10; 5:5; 6:17, 19). This hope is chiefly concerned with the gift of eternal life.[40] Christ is the means and grounds of this hope, certainty of which is grounded in his historic resurrection from the dead (3:16).[41]

The second dimension is *soteriological*. Salvation is a *past* and *present* reality for those who believe (1:15–16; 3:16; 6:12), and it will be the *future* experience of those who persevere, but not of those who wander from the faith (1:19–20; 5:12; 6:10).[42] The "faith" and "hope" aspect of God's plan reflects its futurity, and God's plan to consummate all things in Christ will be realized when he appears (6:14).

The third dimension is *ethical*. The present life matters eschatologically. All life is to be lived in anticipation of divine judgment, from which nothing will be hidden, whether sins or good works[43] (5:24–25; 6:9, 11–14; cf. Luke 12:2; 1 Cor. 4:5; 2 Tim. 1:12, 18; 2:3–7; 4:1, 8). This age is a time of anticipation and preparation.[44] Believers are to hope in God, not wealth (1 Tim. 4:10; 5:5; 6:17), and store up treasure in the coming age through good works (6:18–19; cf. Matt. 6:21; Luke 12:21).

The fourth is *missional*. Christian witness and ministry are undertaken in the conditions of the eschatologically defined "later times" (1 Tim. 4:1) and will conclude only at Christ's return (4:8; 6:14). Thus,

40 See Wieland, *Significance*, 28–33.
41 Wieland, *Significance*, 32; Beale and Gladd, *Hidden but Now Revealed*, 256–57.
42 Young, *Theology*, 70.
43 Towner, *Letters*, 377. See Yarbrough, *Letters*, 298–300.
44 Marshall, *Pastoral Epistles*, 665.

his final appearing in history, in God's own time, creates both assurance and urgency to the activity of mission.[45]

———

Climactic aspects of God's plan lie in the future: Christ Jesus's second appearing, judgment, and the fully realized experience of salvation and eternal life. But God's plan is *by faith*. It is "a faith-based, faith-promoting, faith-operated, and faith-controlled undertaking,"[46] and so, until God's plan is consummated, believers are to persevere in lives of faith and love and truth, with confident expectation in "Christ Jesus our hope" and "God our Savior." The goal is not peaceful coexistence with the world but, rather, as God's household, to live as his people, distinct from the surrounding society, displaying his character, advancing his saving purposes, and so bringing his blessings to the nations.

45 Towner, *Goal*, 73.
46 Kuruvilla, *Timothy, Titus*, 22.

PART 2

---

2 TIMOTHY

Remember Jesus Christ

6

The God of Power

PAUL'S CIRCUMSTANCES HAVE CHANGED since he wrote 1 Timothy. Then, he was expecting to visit Timothy in Ephesus soon (1 Tim. 3:14). Now, he's in chains (2 Tim. 1:8, 16; 4:16), awaiting death (4:6), and asking Timothy to come to him soon (4:9, 13, 21), having been deserted by colleagues (1:15; 4:10, 16) and having endured suffering from enemies (4:14). The finish line is in sight for his earthly life and ministry, and like Moses with Joshua, he needs to entrust God's mission to the next generation.[1] His earlier concern for truth and God's salvation plan is unchanged. But this letter is different. It's not about how God's people are to conduct themselves in God's household but about how Timothy as God's servant (*doulos*, 2:24) is to continue advancing God's saving work in these "last days," with hostility and opposition inside and outside the church (2:14–18, 23–26; 3:1–9, 12–13; 4:3–4).

The reason and the power to do this come from God. So, although this is a deeply personal letter from Paul, coming almost with his dying breath and urgently charging his beloved child to keep the faith and continue his work, it is *God* and *his* work that are central. We see this in the "preponderance of God-language": "God" (*theos*, 13x), "Jesus" (*Iēsous*) and "Christ" (*Christos*) always paired (13x), and "Lord"

---

1   Andreas J. Köstenberger, *Commentary on 1–2 Timothy and Titus*, BTCP (Nashville: Holman Reference, 2017), 530.

(*kyrios*, 16x) for both God and Christ. Fifty-five divine titles, which far outnumber any other noun and account for 4.44 percent of the word count,[2] and that's before including the Holy Spirit (1:7, 14) and divine references without titles (e.g., 1:9, 11, 12)! Paul is departing but *God* will remain; and, as we shall see, Paul's presentation of the triune God serves that truth.[3]

The Saving God of Power

As in 1 Timothy, God's role in salvation dominates the presentation of God, even though the title "Savior" is reserved for Christ Jesus (2 Tim. 1:10). God is the initiator, author, and source of salvation. It is the result of his pretemporal purpose and grace, which "he gave us in Christ Jesus," and made manifest in Christ's appearing (1:9–10). He raised Jesus Christ from the dead[4] and fulfilled his salvation-historical promise of an eternal Davidic King (2:8; cf. 2 Sam. 7:12–16; Isa. 9:6–7; Rom. 1:3–4). He elects people to salvation (2 Tim. 2:10) and grants repentance and saving knowledge of the truth (2:25; cf. 1 Tim. 2:4). He establishes gospel ministry and gives the Spirit to empower it (2 Tim. 1:1, 7–8, 11).[5] His gospel and saving purposes cannot be stopped (2:9–10). His Scriptures make people "wise for salvation" (3:15) and fully equip his people "for every good work" (3:17), including Timothy's work as an evangelist (4:5). God judges the word-ministry of his workers (2:15) and will grant mercy to those who support gospel ministry (1:18b).[6]

In all these ways, past, present, and future, we see God's desire to save (1 Tim. 2:4) and his sovereign and gracious enactment of that plan. For Timothy to follow Paul in the ministry of the gospel is for Timothy to align himself with God's eternal purpose and work. Yet it also means fully investing and being identified with a *crucified* Lord

2   Robert W. Yarbrough, *The Letters to Timothy and Titus*, PNTC (Grand Rapids, MI: Eerdmans, 2018), 13–14.

3   Greg A. Couser, "The Sovereign Savior of 1 and 2 Timothy and Titus," in *EWTG* 107.

4   William D. Mounce, *Pastoral Epistles*, WBC 46 (Nashville: Thomas Nelson, 2000), 512.

5   Chiao Ek Ho, "Mission in the Pastoral Epistles," in *EWTG* 258–59.

6   Köstenberger, *Timothy and Titus*, 224.

(cf. 1 Cor. 1:18–25) and an imprisoned apostle awaiting death (2 Tim. 1:8): in other words, with weakness, suffering, and shame. There's the temptation to hold back and be ashamed.

But God is a God of *power*. Paul develops this important theme with "power" terminology: God has given "us" (i.e., all believers) power (*dynamis*) by his Spirit (1:7).[7] God's power will enable Timothy to join in suffering for the gospel (1:8; cf. Eph. 3:7, 20). God will strengthen (*endynamoō*) Timothy with grace for his ministry (2 Tim. 2:1; cf. Christ, 4:17).[8] God is able (*dynatos*) to guard all that Paul has entrusted to him[9] (1:12; cf. Rom. 4:21); and God's word is able (*dynamai*) to make people "wise for salvation" (2 Tim. 3:15).[10]

God's power is displayed in other ways. He determines the time-table of history, from Christ's appearings to the nature of the times to the moments of our deaths (1:9, 12, 18; 3:1; 4:3, 6, 8). He has power to accomplish his pretemporal plan (1:9–11; 2:8–10). His word cannot be stopped (2:9). His people are a solid foundation irrevocably established by him (2:19).[11] He triumphs over human and spiritual opposition (2:26; 3:8–9). And his power and (related) faithfulness are preeminently displayed in the Christ event—fulfilling his covenant promises to his ancient people—when he raises Jesus from the dead, thereby vindicating his righteous suffering and confirming his eternal messiahship (2:8; cf. Acts 2:25–32).[12]

This powerful God is near to his people. He is our Father (2 Tim. 1:2; cf. 1 Tim. 1:2; Titus 1:4). He saved and called us (2 Tim. 1:9; 2:10). He gives us grace (1:2, 9), mercy (1:16, 18), and peace. He gives us his

7   See Philip H. Towner, *The Letters to Timothy and Titus*, NICNT (Grand Rapids, MI: Eerdmans, 2006), 457–61.

8   I. Howard Marshall, *The Pastoral Epistles*, ICC (Edinburgh: T&T Clark, 1999), 724.

9   George W. Knight, *Commentary on the Pastoral Epistles*, NIGTC (Grand Rapids, MI: Eerdmans, 1992), 379–80; Mounce, *Pastoral Epistles*, 488; Gordon D. Fee, *1 and 2 Timothy, Titus*, NIBC (Peabody, MA: Hendrickson, 1988), 232. See NIV, NASB, ESV footnote.

10 See George Wieland, *The Significance of Salvation: A Study of Salvation Language in the Pastoral Epistles*, PBM (Milton Keynes, UK: Paternoster, 2006), 113, on the use of the verb (*dynamai*) in the "power" theme.

11 Fee, *Timothy, Titus*, 257.

12 See Yarbrough, *Letters*, 376–78.

indwelling Spirit (1:6–7, 14). Knowledge of him gives confidence in adversity (1:12). He speaks to his people by his word (3:15–17; cf. 2:9, 15). He appoints and empowers workers for ministry (1:1, 11; 2:15, 21, 24) and equips them for every good work (1:6–7; 3:17). Like the master of a great house, he sets his people apart as holy to do his will (2:21).[13]

God's strong bond with his people is also in view in two Old Testament citations marking the church as authentically his property (2:19).[14] The first (Num. 16:5 LXX) is drawn from the account of the rebellion of Korah and his companions against Moses. They falsely claimed to represent God and his word, as the opponents in Ephesus are doing. But "the Lord *knows* those who are his," and he does not know *them* as his. They will not succeed (2 Tim. 3:9). However, those God *does* elect and know, and the leaders he appoints, *do* belong to him, and he protects and vindicates them (1:1, 11; 2:14–15; cf. Gal. 4:9). In the second citation (LXX: Isa. 26:13; Num. 16:26–27), we see that God's people are able to call upon him *by name* (cf. Ex. 3:13–15).[15]

This *personal bond* with his people is stressed in the only two titles used for God. He is Father (2 Tim. 1:2) and Lord (*kyrios*, 1:18b; 2:19 [2x], 24), the title used in the LXX to render the Hebrew covenantal name, Yahweh. The bond is of covenantal faithfulness.

Paul and Timothy have firsthand experience of God's presence, faithfulness, and unchanging purposes. Paul serves (*latreuō*) the same God as his ancestors did (1:3; cf. Acts 24:14), who received God's promise of blessing, and "through whom true worship of Yahweh was practiced and transmitted."[16] Timothy belongs to generations of Christian (and Jewish) believers and from childhood was nurtured in God's Old Testament word (2 Tim. 1:5; 3:15; cf. Acts 16:1). He has seen his spiritual father (2 Tim. 1:2) suffer and endure for the gospel and be sustained by the Lord (1:15; 2:9; 3:10–11). Jesus's own Davidic ancestry and experience

---

13 Mounce, *Pastoral Epistles*, 532.
14 Couser, "Sovereign Savior," 128.
15 For "Lord" (*kyrios*) in both citations referring to God. See Köstenberger, *Timothy and Titus*, 224; Luke Timothy Johnson, *The First and Second Letters to Timothy*, AB 35A (New York: Doubleday, 2001), 397.
16 Towner, *Letters*, 449.

of resurrection testify to God's unchanging purposes and fulfillment of his promises (2:8; cf. Ps. 16:8–11; Acts 2:24–32). God does not change or lie (Num. 23:19; Titus 1:2; James 1:17). His redemption plan was established before time and reaches into eternity, and so his past dealings with his chosen people—*and* with those who opposed him—are a source of instruction, courage, and comfort to Timothy and all believers. God knows those who are his, and he is faithful, so they will surely receive his promise of eternal life (2 Tim. 1:1, 12).

Christ Our Risen Savior

In 1 Timothy, the Christological focus is on Christ Jesus's humanity: his coming in the flesh as a man and giving himself in death as a ransom to save sinners (1 Tim. 1:15; 2:6; 3:16; 6:13). Here, reflecting the circumstances and purpose of 2 Timothy—with Paul's approaching death and the suffering and opposition that await believers—the focus is on Christ's resurrection, vindication, rule, power, and eschatological kingdom. Suffering and death have given way to exaltation and life—even Christ's death was the means of *abolishing* death (1:10; 2:11)! Christ is the divine exalted King.

Titles and activities associated with Yahweh in the Old Testament are ascribed to him. He is "Savior" (*sōtēr*, 1:10; cf. Isa. 45:15, 21 LXX; Eph. 5:23; Phil. 3:20; Titus 1:4; 2:13; 3:6) and "Judge" (2 Tim. 4:1, 8; cf. Ps. 7:11). He shares the title "Lord" (*kyrios*) with God (e.g., 2 Tim. 1:18).[17] He receives prayer (1:16, 18a; 4:22) and is the object of eternal worship (4:18).[18] He existed "before the ages began" (1:9). The "epiphany" terminology (*epiphaneia*) that was reserved for Christ's second appearing in 1 Timothy (6:14), and was associated with divine power and intervention in Second Temple Judaism and secular Greek thought, is used here for Christ's first appearing (2 Tim. 1:10;

17 Philip H. Towner, "Christology in the Letters to Timothy and Titus," in *Contours of Christology in the New Testament*, ed. Richard N. Longenecker (Grand Rapids, MI: Eerdmans, 2005), 225, 242.
18 Daniel L. Akin, "The Mystery of Godliness Is Great: Christology in the Pastoral Epistles," in *EWTG* 151.

cf. Titus 2:11; 3:4) *and* his second (2 Tim. 4:1, 8; cf. 1 Tim. 6:14; Titus 2:13), designating his incarnation and earthly ministry as a divine saving intervention.[19] In fact, the very notion of appearing implies preexistence, which is "an attribute of deity."[20] Christ and his work are so closely aligned and intertwined with the person and work of God (the Father) that in some texts it's difficult to know whether the first or second person of the Godhead is in view, with trusted interpreters opting for different answers.[21]

This exegetical quandary particularly arises with several occurrences of the title "Lord." I've already interpreted some as referring to God when other interpreters opt for Christ (2 Tim. 1:18b; 2:19 [2x], 24).[22] Other occurrences seem more clearly to refer to Christ (1:8, 16, 18a; 2:7; 4:8), and some might refer to God—as Father or in his triunity— or Christ (2:22; 3:11; 4:14, 17–18, 22).[23] Either way, the title's use in the LXX and here for both God and Christ (*and* the ambiguity in its referent) make a strong statement of Christ's divinity. Besides, even if the referent of the title remains unclear in some texts, in truth, little hangs on the distinction, given the unity in being, purpose, and work of the divine persons (see e.g., 1:1, 9–10).

This unity is especially seen in salvation. God "saved us and called us," yet Christ Jesus is "our Savior" (1:9–10). God's promise of eternal life "is in Christ Jesus" (1:1), and his saving grace was given "in Christ Jesus" before the ages began. The salvation blessings of "grace, mercy, and peace" come from the Father and Christ Jesus (1:2; 2:1). Christ's appearings (1:10; 4:1, 8) are the heart of God's soteriological project.

---

19 Towner, "Christology," 225; Andrew Y. Lau, *Manifest in the Flesh: The Epiphany Christology of the Pastoral Epistles*, WUNT 2.86 (Tübingen: Mohr Siebeck, 1996), 118–19.

20 Towner, "Christology," 225.

21 E.g., 2 Tim. 1:12: referring to God (Mounce, *Pastoral Epistles*, 487; Abraham Kuruvilla, *1 & 2 Timothy, Titus: A Theological Commentary for Preachers* [Eugene, OR: Cascade, 2021], 149; Köstenberger, *Timothy and Titus*, 219; Towner, *Letters*, 475, but footnote "or possibly Christ"); Christ (Gerald L. Bray, *The Pastoral Epistles*, ITC [London: T&T Clark, 2019], 338); uncertain (Fee, *Timothy, Titus*, 231, "probably 'God,' perhaps 'Christ' "; Marshall, *Pastoral Epistles*, 710, "either God or, perhaps more probably, Christ").

22 So, Towner, *Letters*, 484, 532–35, 546.

23 See Yarbrough, *Letters*, 23.

Christ's first appearing marked the turning of the ages such that God's
eternal purpose has "now" (*nyn*) been made visible and accomplished
in history *in Christ* and continues to be made known through the gospel
about him (1:10). Christ's second appearing will end this epoch, when
he appears again on that eschatological "day" (1:12, 18; 4:1, 8) as the
appointed Judge of "the living and the dead" (4:1) to grant mercy from
God (*para kyriou*, 1:18b), to reward the faithful (4:8, 18), and to repay
evil (4:14). Even now, Christ grants mercy to those partnering in gospel
ministry (1:16)[24] and evaluates gospel work as a commanding officer
(2:3–4) and co-witness with God (4:1).

While, in his first appearing, Christ took on our humanity and
weakness, and knew shame, suffering, and death (1:8; 2:3, 8, 11; cf. 4:16
with Ps. 22[25]), the emphasis in 2 Timothy is on Christ's *triumph* over
death. In fact, the two brief references to his death stress *life*: he has
been *raised* from the dead (2:8); and if we have died with him, we will
live with him (2:11). He has "abolished death and brought life and
immortality to light" (1:10). He has an *eternal* heavenly kingdom (4:1,
18). His salvation brings eternal glory (2:10). Death is no obstacle to
him: it does not allow anyone to escape his righteous judgment (4:1;
cf. Acts 10:42) or prevent him from recognizing or rewarding faithful
service (2 Tim. 4:6–8). Even his *human* ancestry identifies him as the
fulfillment of God's messianic promise of an *eternal* Davidic kingship
(2:8; cf. 2 Sam. 7:12–16; Jer. 33:17; Luke 1:33).[26] As Robert Yarbrough
explains: "Victory is in Jesus's earthly bloodline, despite the suffering
that ended his life. As ruler over all, including death, Christ in David's
lineage receives the kingdom promised to his forebear."[27] Death will
be the last enemy he destroys, but even now, King Jesus has overcome
death (John 11:25; 1 Cor. 15:56–57).

So the opponents' mistake was not that they taught about resurrection per se but that they taught that, for believers, it had *already*

24 Mounce, *Pastoral Epistles*, 495.
25 Towner, *Letters*, 638–41.
26 Marshall, *Pastoral Epistles*, 734–35.
27 Yarbrough, *Letters*, 377.

happened (2 Tim. 2:18). At best, their (so-called) resurrection was a purely spiritual affair, which effectively denied the bodily resurrection of Jesus and future bodily resurrection to life of those who trust in him (cf. Dan. 12:2; 1 Cor. 15:12–23).[28] It was a poor imitation of Christ's victory over death! His resurrection was *bodily*, and through it he abolished death and brought life and *bodily* immortality to light.

This risen, living Christ is near to those he saves. He is *"our* Lord" (2 Tim. 1:8) and *"our* Savior" (1:10). Believers call on him (2:22). "The Lord," probably Christ, has rescued and will rescue Paul from trials (3:11) and has "stood with" Paul, has strengthened him, and did not abandon him, as everyone else did when Paul was brought before a human court (4:16–17).[29] Timothy is to share in suffering for the gospel with Paul *and Christ* (1:8; 2:3).[30] Paul prays that Timothy would, like him, know the Lord's presence and strengthening (4:22; cf. Rom. 8:16). And Christ's union with his people is such that if we have died with him, we will live with him (Rom. 6:8) and reign with him (2 Tim. 2:11–12; cf. Rom. 8:17; Eph. 2:5–6).

The logic is that if Timothy follows Paul in persevering and suffering for the gospel, he will not tread that path alone: Christ Jesus, the resurrected, vindicated Lord and King, who himself trod that path and abolished death and provided life and immortality, will be *with* Timothy to strengthen him, rescue him, and bring him safely into Christ's eternal kingdom—as Christ has done and will do for Paul, and also for all who long for Christ's second appearing.

The Spirit of Power

The Holy Spirit is less prominent in 2 Timothy than in some of Paul's other letters, but the work of the Spirit is still vital to the letter's message. The Spirit indwells believers (1:14), empowers them for life and min-

---

28 See Dillon T. Thornton, *Hostility in the House of God: An Investigation of the Opponents in 1 and 2 Timothy*, BBRSup 15 (Winona Lake, IN: Eisenbrauns, 2016), 181–86.

29 Marshall, *Pastoral Epistles*, 824.

30 In these texts, Paul uses a series of compound verbs with *syn-* prefixes, meaning "together with," which stress union with Christ. Yarbrough, *Letters*, 359n46; Kuruvilla, *Timothy, Titus*, 146n15, 161.

istry (1:6–7), and inspires and preserves the word of God through which salvation in Christ is attained by faith (1:14; 3:16). That is, the Holy Spirit continues his work begun at Pentecost, mediating God's presence and power to individual believers and the church to make God's salvation in Christ known (Acts 1:8; 2:4, 17–18). And as all believers share a common experience of the one Spirit, so too there is only one true apostolic deposit that the Spirit preserves (2 Tim. 1:14).[31]

The Spirit's presence and work in believers is an experience of Trinitarian grace. He is "the gift *of God*,"[32] given *by God* to "us"—that is, Paul, Timothy, and all believers[33] (1:6–7; cf. 1 Cor. 2:12), who indwells believers personally (2 Tim. 1:6; cf. 2 Cor. 1:22) and corporately[34] (2 Tim. 1:14; cf. 1 Cor. 3:16). The Spirit is holy (2 Tim. 1:14) as God is holy (1 Pet. 1:16) and calls believers to "a holy calling" (2 Tim. 1:9). The Spirit gives and produces in us the fruit of faith—not cowardice but power (Eph. 3:16), love, and self-control (2 Tim. 1:7), and will empower Timothy and all God's people not to be ashamed of Christ or his apostle, and to suffer for the gospel (1:8; cf. 2:1).[35]

By contrast, those who love pleasure and not God have a form of godliness (*eusebeia*) but lack its power (*dynamis*, 3:5): they are without the Spirit.[36] As Towner explains: "It is the very presence of the Spirit in the life of the community and the observable characteristics of the life he produces in God's people that promises suffering. What the Spirit provides is power to endure the stress that comes from bearing witness to God, not removal to some safe place."[37]

---

31 Bray, *Pastoral Epistles*, 344.
32 Towner, *Letters*, 457–61.
33 Gordon D. Fee, *God's Empowering Presence: The Holy Spirit in the Letters of Paul* (Peabody, MA: Hendrickson, 1994), 795.
34 Yarbrough, *Letters*, 366; Bray, *Pastoral Epistles*, 344.
35 Fee, *Empowering Presence*, 785.
36 Fee, *Empowering Presence*, 793. Thornton, *Hostility*, 203.
37 Towner, *Letters*, 466.

Paul is confident that both he and Timothy will be fully equipped and empowered to face the challenges of gospel ministry that lie ahead, with false teaching and opposition inside and outside the church. His confidence is based on the character, eternal purposes, and saving work of the Trinitarian God, who is supremely powerful and always present with his people—the giver of grace and mercy, love and life, who has triumphed over the grave.

Whatever trials await Paul and Timothy, and all those who believe, they will occur between the two appearings of Christ Jesus, the vindicated, risen, messianic King, who has abolished death and won life and immortality for the elect, and who will return as the righteous Judge of the living and the dead.

7

The Promise of Life

IN HIS FIRST LETTER TO TIMOTHY, Paul's treatment of salvation focused on its universal scope in the face of exclusivist and ascetic false teaching. Here in 2 Timothy, with Paul on death row and Timothy being called to join him in suffering for the gospel, the pressing question is, How sure is God's eternal salvation when, in this life, those who believe, especially those in gospel ministry, face trials and persecution?

The answer lies in God's pretemporal plan and the revelation and enactment of that plan in history in Christ's appearings. In particular, Paul's presentation of salvation is weighted toward the eschatological future, when God's redemptive work already accomplished in Christ will, at his return, assuredly issue in eternal life, immortality, indestructibility, and future reward for those who believe and faithfully persevere. It is the firm and glorious promise of eternal life in the face of—and beyond—physical death.

The Provision of Salvation

God is the author, initiator, and source of salvation. It is the outworking of his pretemporal purpose and grace, the realization of what he established and gave "us" before time (1:9–10). Paul and Christian believers might face opposition and suffer harm, and some might be faithless, but nothing can threaten God's salvation plan.

It is underwritten by his eternal sovereign purpose. He remains faithful (2:13).[1]

Salvation comes through Christ Jesus, "our Savior." In his first appearing (*epiphaneia*)—his life, death, resurrection, and ascension—he destroyed death and brought life and immortality to light (1:9–10; 2:8; cf. 1 Tim. 3:16), inaugurating the present age when salvation may be attained through the good news of him (2 Tim. 1:11; cf. 2 Cor. 6:2). His second appearing will bring its consummation, when he will appear as Judge (2 Tim. 4:1, 8, 14) to grant mercy from God (1:18)[2] and safely bring the elect into his heavenly kingdom (4:18).

Seven "in Christ Jesus" statements further highlight the Christological nature of salvation: the promise of eternal life is in Christ (1:1); God's saving purpose and grace were given in or through Christ (1:9);[3] eternal salvation is in Christ (2:10); the Old Testament Scriptures teach that salvation comes through faith in Christ (3:15); the "faith and love" of Christian existence come from him (1:13);[4] grace that is in Christ provides strength for gospel ministry (2:1); and faith in him is the source of godly living (3:12).[5] That is, every aspect of salvation is found in Christ, and Christian existence comes from being united *with him*. If we have died with him—to self and sin, and even in physical death (Gal. 2:20; Phil. 3:10–11)[6]—we will live *with him*; and if we endure *with him*, we will reign *with him* (2 Tim. 2:11–12; cf. Rom. 5:17; 6:8); living and reigning in the present even as we long for his appearing and full resurrection life (2 Tim. 4:8; cf. 2:18).[7]

---

1   See Gordon D. Fee, *1 and 2 Timothy, Titus*, NIBC (Peabody, MA: Hendrickson, 1988), 251.
2   William D. Mounce, *Pastoral Epistles*, WBC 46 (Nashville: Thomas Nelson, 2000), 496.
3   I. Howard Marshall, *The Pastoral Epistles*, ICC (Edinburgh: T&T Clark, 1999), 706.
4   Gerald L. Bray, *The Pastoral Epistles*, ITC (London: T&T Clark, 2019), 342.
5   Philip H. Towner, *The Letters to Timothy and Titus*, NICNT (Grand Rapids, MI: Eerdmans, 2006), 578.
6   Fee, *Timothy, Titus*, 249.
7   Robert W. Yarbrough, *The Letters to Timothy and Titus*, PNTC (Grand Rapids, MI: Eerdmans, 2018), 380–81; Fee, *Timothy, Titus*, 249–50.

No wonder the doxological climax of the letter ascribes eternal glory to the Lord Christ Jesus[8] as the divine agent of God's glorious eternal salvation (4:18; cf. Rom. 9:5; 1 Tim. 1:11, 17; 2 Tim. 2:10; Titus 2:13).

The Recipients of Salvation

Salvation is entirely the gift of God's grace. It does not depend on human initiative, effort, or merit (2 Tim. 1:9). It is by God's plan and grace given "to us"—Paul, Timothy, and all believers[9]—before time (or we) began. God chose. God saved. God called. Under the old covenant, the children of Israel as his elect people experienced his salvation and blessing. Now, his "elect" (*eklektoi*, 2:10; cf. 2:19; Col. 3:12; Titus 1:1)[10] are Jews and Gentiles, both beneficiaries of his eternal purpose to save a people for himself, not because of their own righteousness but according to his grace and mercy (2 Tim. 1:2, 5; 4:17; cf. Deut. 9:4–6; Titus 3:5).

Salvation, then, is by faith (*pistis*, 2 Tim. 1:5, 12; 2:18; 3:14) in what God has done in Christ (1:12; 3:15). It is knowledge of the truth (3:7; cf. 1 Tim. 2:4) that comes only through hearing and believing God's word (2 Tim. 2:8; 3:15; 4:17; cf. Rom. 10:17). This is why word ministry is so crucial to God's salvation project (2 Tim. 1:1, 11; 2:15; 4:2) and why the opponents must be corrected or avoided (2:14, 16–18, 23–26; 3:5, 13; 4:3–4, 14–15).

Second Timothy does not have a statement that, like 1 Timothy 1:15, identifies sin as the reason for our universal need of salvation. The focus is on the actual sins besetting the church: on apostasy and false teachers, who are the embodiment for everything contrary to faith and godliness. As in 1 Timothy, they break God's Old Testament law (2 Tim. 3:2–3; cf. Ex. 20:12, 16–17; 1 Tim. 1:9–10; 4:1–3). But more starkly, these people break the greatest commandment: they love self, money, and pleasure,

8 George W. Knight, *Commentary on the Pastoral Epistles*, NIGTC (Grand Rapids, MI: Eerdmans, 1992), 473; Marshall, *Pastoral Epistles*, 826.
9 Yarbrough, *Letters*, 360.
10 Fee, *Timothy, Titus*, 247.

not *God* (2 Tim. 3:2, 4; cf. Deut. 6:5; Matt. 22:36–40). And they break the second great commandment to love one's neighbor as oneself: they teach error and are proud, arrogant, abusive, brutal, and divisive (2 Tim. 2:16, 23; 3:2–4, 13). They have a pretense of godliness but lack the power of God's Spirit (3:5).[11] Instead, they're captives doing the devil's work in a spiritual war (2:26)—evil, deceived deceivers (3:13), who take others captive, including certain weak women, burdened by past "sins" (*hamartia*, 3:6) and ruled by worldly passions (2:22; Titus 3:3),[12] and thus vulnerable to their teaching.[13]

Increasing godlessness and spiritual opposition, and the rising tide of apostasy as people abandon God's apostle and the gospel and deny Christ (2 Tim. 1:15; 4:3–4, 10, 14–16; cf. 1 Tim. 1:20; 4:1),[14] are prophesied features of these eschatological "last days" (2 Tim. 3:1; 4:3; cf. Mark 13).[15] Hence the warning "If we disown him, he will also disown us" (2 Tim. 2:12 NIV; cf. Matt. 10:33). Yet it is still possible to be brought back from the brink by God—even those taken captive by the devil might be granted repentance and saving knowledge of the truth (2 Tim. 2:25–26; cf. 2:21).

And the need for repentance and transformation doesn't end with conversion. Believers must continue to depart from unrighteousness (*adikia*, 2:19).[16] Timothy is to "*flee* youthful passions and *pursue* righteousness, faith, love, and peace," and make himself useful to God (2:22; cf. 1 Tim. 6:11). All those who call upon God from a pure heart must do the same (2 Tim. 2:21). God called us with a "holy calling" (1:9) and indwells us by his Holy Spirit (1:14). His people are to be holy as he is (Lev. 19:2).[17]

---

11 Towner, *Letters*, 560.

12 Paul's obvious esteem for other women even in this letter shows that this observation does not come from a sexist or misogynistic mindset (2 Tim. 1:5; 3:14–15; 4:19–21).

13 Towner, *Letters*, 562–63.

14 Towner, *Letters*, 603.

15 Marshall, *Pastoral Epistles*, 769–71.

16 Knight, *Pastoral Epistles*, 416.

17 Donald Guthrie, *The Pastoral Epistles*, TNTC (1957; repr., Leicester: Inter-Varsity Press, 1984), 129.

Salvation *When*, *to What*, and *from What*?

The timeline of salvation extends from the eternal past to future eternity. It is portrayed as a "complete act in the *past*" when God saved and called his people (2 Tim. 1:9; cf. Eph. 2:5, 8; Titus 3:5);[18] as the *present* experience of believers (2 Tim. 1:10; 2:25; cf. 1 Cor. 15:2), who now "live" with Christ, are indwelt by the Spirit and enjoy the blessings of salvation (2 Tim. 1:2, 7, 13–14, 16; 2:1, 7; 4:17); and as a *future* experience of "eternal glory" and eternal life in Christ's heavenly kingdom (1:1; 2:10; 4:1, 18).

Christ's two appearings are the decisive turning points on that timeline. The first has ushered in the present epoch when salvation is attained and Christian existence is lived out; and then the end of this age is when he appears on "that day" (1:12, 18; 4:8; cf. Phil. 1:6; 2 Thess. 1:10) and believers receive the full realization of their salvation, of resurrection life, reign, and glory (2 Tim. 2:11–12). Though now they look to the *promise* of life (1:1), immortality and indestructibility will be theirs *fully experienced* (1:10; cf. 1 Cor. 15:50–54). Little wonder they long for his appearing (2 Tim. 4:8)!

God's salvation answers the two great problems facing humanity resulting from our sinful rebellion against him: death and judgment (Gen. 2:17; 3:6, 22–24; Rom. 6:23). Second Timothy doesn't explore the reasons we face these, but Paul demonstrates from his own life that they are no longer to be feared.

He faces imminent physical death but still proclaims the "promise of the life that is in Christ Jesus" (1:1) and expects the Lord to bring him "safely into his heavenly kingdom" (4:18) to live and reign with Christ with eternal glory (2:10–12). The reason for Paul's confidence is that Christ rendered death inoperative through his resurrection from the dead (1:10; 2:8; cf. Rom. 6:10).[19] So, although the resurrection of believers hasn't yet occurred (2 Tim. 2:18), the bodily resurrection of Jesus has! Paul has entrusted his life to God and has full confidence

18 Marshall, *Pastoral Epistles*, 704.
19 George Wieland, *The Significance of Salvation: A Study of Salvation Language in the Pastoral Epistles*, PBM (Milton Keynes, UK: Paternoster, 2006), 123.

that God will guard it until the day of Christ's return and reign (1:12).[20] He knows that physical death is a "departure," not the end (4:6).

In terms of judgment, Paul's circumstances again strain against eschatological realities. He is on trial before human courts (4:16–18),[21] but his attention is on the eschatological divine courtroom, when all "the living and the dead" will be judged (4:1; cf. Acts 10:42; 2 Cor. 5:10). That is when true and eternal justice will be found. Then, all those who have persevered and longed for Christ's appearing will receive "the crown of righteousness" (*dikaiosynēs*) that awaits them, awarded by the righteous (*dikaios*) Judge (2 Tim. 4:8; cf. James 1:12; Rev. 2:10).[22] Whether this crown is itself (the full experience of) righteousness (Gal. 5:5)[23] or a reward, such as eternal life, as "the fitting recompense for a righteous life"[24] (see 2 Tim. 3:16) or both,[25] gaining this award requires training, hardship, striving according to the rules, and perseverance to the end, as the athletic and military imagery suggests (2:5; 4:7).[26]

This victory wreath is also vindication for suffering and shame endured in service of the gospel (e.g., Onesiphorus, 1:16–18). Those who *oppose* the gospel will receive their due reward too (4:10, 14; cf. Col. 4:14; Philem. 24).[27] In the courtroom that counts, those who love Christ and serve the gospel will be acquitted, vindicated, and rewarded. Those who don't, will not.

The Climax of Salvation History

Finally, Paul, Timothy, and all believers can have certainty about the salvation found in Christ because it is the climax of salvation

---

20 Knight, *Pastoral Epistles*, 380.
21 See Abraham Kuruvilla, *1 & 2 Timothy, Titus: A Theological Commentary for Preachers* (Eugene, OR: Cascade, 2021), 192n27.
22 Marshall, *Pastoral Epistles*, 809.
23 Fee, *Timothy and Titus*, 290; Knight, *Pastoral Epistles*, 615; Kuruvilla, *Timothy, Titus*, 190.
24 J. N. D. Kelly, *The Pastoral Epistles: I & II Timothy, Titus* (London: Black, 1963), 210.
25 Towner, *Letters*, 616; Yarbrough, *Letters*, 445.
26 William B. Barcley, "2 Timothy," in *BTINT* 389.
27 Knight, *Pastoral Epistles*, 464.

history. Only its consummation remains. God's eternal purpose to save a people for himself has been accomplished in history through Christ Jesus (2 Tim. 1:9–10), God's promised messianic King (2:8; cf. 2 Sam. 7), who is with his people (2 Tim. 2:11–12; cf. Isa. 7:14) and reigns over an eternal kingdom (2 Tim. 2:10, 12; 4:1, 18; cf. Isa. 9:6–7).

Accordingly, Paul stresses the continuity between the old and new covenants even as he stresses the superiority and finality of God's saving work in Christ. Paul's and Timothy's Jewish ancestors worshiped the God of the gospel (2 Tim. 1:3, 5). The Jewish Scriptures, rightly understood, teach salvation in Christ (3:15). Yahweh's promises to his ancient people are reapplied to Christian believers, assuring them of God's election, knowledge, and covenant fidelity (2:19).[28] And his people now can learn lessons from salvation history. God still demands that his people "depart from iniquity" (2:19; cf. Isa. 26:13). He still has opponents (2 Tim. 2:18–19; 3:8; cf. Ex. 7:11; Num. 16:5).[29] The faithful servant is still a "man/person of God" (*theou anthrōpos*, 2 Tim. 3:17; cf. Deut. 33:1; Josh. 14:6; 1 Tim. 6:11).[30] Moses and Joshua serve as a pattern for Paul and Timothy (2 Tim. 1:6; 2:1, 24; cf. Num. 27:18–23; Deut. 31:6–7; 34:5).[31] God's earlier vindication of his servants serves as a pattern (2 Tim. 2:8; 4:17; cf. Ps. 22). Above all, salvation history shows that, despite all opposition, evil, and apostasy, God's plan progresses and succeeds (2 Tim. 2:13; cf. Gen. 50:20; Ezek. 34). His opponents might overturn[32] the faith of some, but "they will not get very far" (2 Tim. 2:18; 3:9).

But there is also wonderful discontinuity. Now, in Christ, God's Abrahamic promises of blessing flowing to all nations through

---

28 Philip H. Towner, "1–2 Timothy and Titus," in *Commentary on the New Testament Use of the Old Testament*, ed. G. K. Beale and D. A. Carson (Grand Rapids, MI: Baker Academic, 2007), 906.
29 Towner, "Timothy and Titus," 907.
30 See Marshall, *Pastoral Epistles*, 656, 796.
31 Andreas J. Köstenberger, *Commentary on Timothy and Titus*, BTCP (Nashville: Holman Reference, 2017), 530.
32 See HCSB; Fee, *Timothy, Titus*, 257.

God's chosen one have been fulfilled (Gen. 12:1–3; Rev. 5:9). Now, eternal redemption into his heavenly kingdom is offered to all peoples through faith in the one gospel, which must be proclaimed throughout the world (2 Tim. 4:17; cf. Matt. 28:19; Luke 24:47; 1 Tim. 2:7; 2 Tim. 1:11; 2:9).

8

The Living Word

THE CERTAINTY OF GOD'S ETERNAL SALVATION is one reason Paul can urge his beloved child to follow in his footsteps as a faithful servant of the gospel. A second reason is the word of God itself.

God's word—written and spoken, ancient and apostolic—is a key feature of 2 Timothy. It is even portrayed as a living being (2:9; 3:16)! If Timothy grasps the nature of God's word—its truth, power, and sufficiency—he will know that God's plan of salvation can only succeed and that, through God's word, Timothy will be empowered and fully equipped for his word-based ministry and able to endure the shame and suffering it brings.

The Apostolic Word

As is his practice, Paul uses several overlapping terms for the body of content associated with his apostolic ministry, each of which highlights different aspects of that content.

The Apostolic Gospel

The important term "gospel" (*euangelion*) occurs only once in 1 Timothy, as "the gospel of the glory of the blessed God," with which Paul had been entrusted (1 Tim. 1:11). Here in 2 Timothy, the term occurs three times, in relation to two summaries of God's saving work in Christ (1:8–10; 2:8). The good news of the gospel is this: (1) God saved and called his elect, not because of our own merit but because of his purpose and grace, which he gave us in Christ in eternity past; (2) this salvation plan has now been revealed and accomplished in the appearing of our Savior, Christ Jesus, in history; and (3) he is God's promised messianic Savior, whom God raised from the dead, and who destroyed death and made eternal life and glory possible and available to all who believe the gospel.

The gospel is "the word *of God*" (*ho logos tou theou*, 2:9). He is its source and power. It is "the promise of the life that is in Christ Jesus" (1:1):[1] a dynamic, life-giving, living power that brings salvation and eternal life (2:10; cf. Isa. 55:10–11; Acts 6:7). Despite the forces arrayed against gospel messengers (2 Tim. 2:9; 3:10–11) and God's people generally (3:12), the word of God cannot be bound, and nothing can stop it from doing what he purposed from eternity past.

The good news and its proclamation are closely associated with Paul's apostolic ministry *and* with suffering. He was appointed by God as a herald, apostle, and teacher *for the gospel* (1:10–11; cf. 1 Tim. 2:7; 2 Tim. 1:1); he preaches "*my* [Paul's] gospel" (2 Tim. 2:8; cf. Rom. 2:16); he suffers as a prisoner *because of* (2 Tim. 1:12)[2] and *for the gospel* (2:9); and Timothy is to join him in suffering *for the sake of the gospel* (1:8; 2:3; 4:5).[3] And yet, Paul doesn't shrink back. He's not ashamed of the gospel or the dishonor and suffering it brings (1:8, 12; cf. Rom. 1:16). Rather, he endures everything so the gospel can spread and the elect be saved (2 Tim. 2:10; cf. 1 Cor. 9:19–23). Timothy, likewise, is to proclaim the gospel (2 Tim. 4:2, 5) and not be ashamed of bearing witness (*martyrion*)[4] about Christ (1:8; cf. 1 Tim. 2:6). Gospel proclamation and suffering go hand in hand, but the progress of the gospel isn't stopped.

This is on display in Paul's trial. We might have thought this was a defeat for the progress of the gospel, but instead, Paul, as a God-appointed "herald" (*kēryx*, 2 Tim. 1:11 NIV) of the gospel, was empowered by

---

1   Philip H. Towner, *The Letters to Timothy and Titus*, NICNT (Grand Rapids, MI: Eerdmans, 2006), 442.

2   George W. Knight, *Commentary on the Pastoral Epistles*, NIGTC (Grand Rapids, MI: Eerdmans, 1992), 378.

3   I. Howard Marshall, *The Pastoral Epistles*, ICC (Edinburgh: T&T Clark, 1999), 703.

4   Marshall, *Pastoral Epistles*, 702.

Christ to proclaim the message (*kērygma*) fully, so that all those in at-
tendance—the authorities and cosmopolitan crowd—heard the gospel,
such that Paul could say that through him *all* the Gentiles heard (4:17;
cf. Acts 1:8; 1 Tim. 2:7; 3:16).[5] He had finished the race (2 Tim. 4:7).

Apostolic Teaching

Together with the gospel proper, the apostolic message ("words,"[6] *logoi*,
4:15) includes gospel-related instruction addressing belief, doctrine,
and the Christian life: "the pattern of the sound words" Timothy heard
from Paul (1:13; 2:2); "the deposit" Paul entrusted to him (*parathēkē*,
1:14; cf. 1 Tim. 6:20); and Paul's/sound "teaching" (*didaskalia*, 2 Tim.
3:10; 4:3; cf. 3:16).

As in 1 Timothy, these different terms foreground different aspects
of the content. As "words," it has been and can be communicated. As
"a pattern of sound words," it signals not a creedal fixed form of words
but the stable and fixed nature of "a coherent body of instruction,"[7] for
which Paul's words were an accurate and reliable guide.[8] As a precious
"deposit," the content is to be guarded and preserved, with the enabling
power of the Holy Spirit. And as "teaching," the educational grounds
of Christian faith and practice are in view, where salvation involves
coming to a knowledge of the truth (2 Tim. 2:25; 3:7; cf. 1 Tim. 2:4;
Titus 1:1).

This content is apostolic (2 Tim. 1:11; 3:10), "good" (1:14), "faithful" (*pistos*, 2:11),[9] "the truth" (*alētheia*, 2:15, 25; 3:7; 4:4), and "sound/
healthy" (*hygiainō*, 1:13; 4:3). The opponents, however, opposed the
word (*logos*) of truth (2:15, 18; 3:8) and quarreled about words (2:14).
Their message (*logos*) and the speed and effect of its spread were like

5   Towner, *Letters*, 642–43; J. N. D. Kelly, *The Pastoral Epistles: I & II Timothy, Titus* (London:
    Black, 1963), 219.
6   NKJV, HCSB, NET.
7   Andreas J. Köstenberger, *Commentary on 1–2 Timothy and Titus*, BTCP (Nashville: Hol-
    man Reference, 2017), 220n52.
8   Towner, *Letters*, 477.
9   See Luke Timothy Johnson, *The First and Second Letters to Timothy*, AB 35A (New York:
    Doubleday, 2001), 381.

gangrene, bringing disease, not health, to the faith of their hearers (2:14, 16–18).[10]

Timothy's ministry is to be defined by and devoted to the apostolic word. He is to "*join in suffering* for the gospel" (1:8; 2:3); "*follow* the pattern of the sound words" (1:13); "*guard* the good deposit" (1:14); "*entrust*" these things (2:2); "*remind* them of these things" (2:14); "*avoid* irreverent babble" (2:16, 23); "*continue*" in what he has learned (3:14); "*preach* the word," "be *ready*," "*reprove, rebuke,* and *exhort*" (4:2); "*do* the work of an evangelist" and "*fulfill* [his] ministry" (4:5).[11] The ability to teach well is essential to his task (2:24; cf. 1 Tim. 3:2; 2 Tim. 2:2). But he will not be on his own. He is to multiply word workers (2 Tim. 2:2).

More importantly, his task is *God's* mission. Servants of the word are workers and bondservants *of God* (2:15, 24). Their ministry is conducted before, and will be judged by, *God and Christ* (1:16, 18; 2:14–15; 4:1). *God* provides the divine enabling power to guard and teach the word (1:7–8, 14; 2:1–2). *God* grants the fruit of teaching and correcting, even in the toughest cases (2:25–26). *God's* Holy Scriptures fully equip *his* people for every good work, especially word ministry (3:16–17).[12] And *Christ's* appearing, kingdom, and judgment provide the context and rationale for word ministry (4:1–2). Timothy and other faithful people (*pistois anthrōpois,* 2:2)[13] are to preserve, protect, promote, and multiply the apostolic word, but *God* will make it happen.

The Word of God Written

Paul directs Timothy to, and makes use of, a further source of authoritative teaching: the written word of God, seen in the parallel terms,[14] "the sacred writings" (*hiera grammata,* 3:15) and "all Scripture" (*pasa graphē,* 3:16). This forms one of two classic New Testament statements about

---

10 Abraham Kuruvilla, *1 & 2 Timothy, Titus: A Theological Commentary for Preachers* (Eugene, OR: Cascade, 2021), 168–69.

11 Words in italics are imperatives.

12 Robert W. Yarbrough, *The Letters to Timothy and Titus,* PNTC (Grand Rapids, MI: Eerdmans, 2018), 432–33.

13 NET, NASB, NRSV; Towner, *Letters,* 491.

14 Knight, *Pastoral Epistles,* 445.

Scripture (3:15–17; 2 Pet. 1:19–21). Paul wants Timothy to *continue* in what he has learned and believed (2 Tim. 3:14), and for that he, and the church, need to grasp the divine provision of the Scriptures. No believer, even less those entrusted with gospel ministry, need be unprepared or inadequately equipped (3:17; cf. 2:2), even in the absence of Paul.

Several aspects of the dense statement in 3:14–17 need teasing out.[15]

First, what is the identity of "the sacred writings" and "all Scripture"? The "sacred writings," with which Timothy had been acquainted since childhood, is a technical term for the Old Testament, or Hebrew Scriptures (1:5; cf. Acts 16:1).[16] "All Scripture" could refer to that same collection, but it's more likely that Paul uses "all" to broaden the reference. In 1 Timothy, he called the (written) words of Jesus "Scripture" (*graphē*, 5:18). Elsewhere, Paul expected his letters to be treated like Scripture—namely, read, studied, shared, and obeyed (1 Cor. 14:37; Col. 4:16; 1 Thess. 5:27; 2 Thess. 2:15), and Peter calls Paul's letters "Scripture" (*graphas*, 2 Pet. 3:15–16). The different terminology, then, likely marks a shift from an Old Testament designation for God's written word to a broader term that embraces apostolic writings.[17]

Second, note the continuity of the Old Testament with the apostolic gospel. The Hebrew Scriptures of Timothy's childhood, when rightly interpreted, directed "those taught by [them] to faith in Christ and a life of righteousness, and hence to salvation"[18] (2 Tim. 3:15; e.g., Isa. 53; cf. Luke 24:25–27; Rom. 15:4; 1 Cor. 10:11). There is unity in the message of the Old Testament and apostolic gospel. Salvation in Christ is at the heart of both.

Third, Timothy learned the word of God not in isolation but in relationships where he had shared personal history with his instructors (2 Tim. 1:5; 3:10, 14–15; cf. Phil. 4:9), both men and women (at least,

15 For detailed discussion of the exegetical and hermeneutical considerations, see Knight, *Pastoral Epistles*, 445–48; William D. Mounce, *Pastoral Epistles*, WBC 46 (Nashville: Thomas Nelson, 2000), 565–70.

16 Köstenberger, *Timothy and Titus*, 410n161.

17 Knight, *Pastoral Epistles*, 448.

18 George Wieland, *The Significance of Salvation: A Study of Salvation Language in the Pastoral Epistles*, PBM (Milton Keynes, UK: Paternoster, 2006), 165.

Paul, Lois, and Eunice). Timothy's knowledge of their godly lives and doctrine was reason for continuing in what he had learned from them, unlike the conduct and teaching of the opponents (2 Tim. 3:8, 13). In faith and learning, he belonged to the historic community of the Lord's people (1:3–5).

Fourth, consider the two predicative adjectives "God-breathed and useful." The first term (*theopneustos*) is a compound of "God" (*theos*) and "blow, breathe on" (*pneō*), and occurs only here in the New Testament.[19] It is describing not the experience of Scripture's authors or its effect on those who hear it but the God-breathed nature of the text itself. The second attribute is a direct consequence of the first. Scripture is profitable and beneficial *because* it comes from God. He is its source and life and power and wisdom.

Fifth, *all* Scripture, ancient and apostolic, in every part, is God-breathed and profitable. This is not true of *some* Scriptures and not others; rather there is *no Scripture* that is not like this.[20] "This is another way of saying that scripture is God's word"[21] (see John 10:35), and as God's word, it is true and useful for teaching, rebuking, correcting, and training in righteousness.[22]

Sixth, Scripture is useful for positive and negative instruction. "Teaching" (*didaskalia*) and "training [*paideia*] in righteousness" increase people's knowledge and love of God and his truth and produce godly living. "Rebuking and correcting" are remedial activities that seek to turn people from ungodly living and doctrinal error and set them right. The usefulness of Scripture lies in its ability to transform lives.

Seventh, Scripture is God-breathed in order that the "person [*anthrōpos*] of God" (AT) may be fully prepared and equipped for every good work, which includes these activities of word ministry (2 Tim. 3:17). That is, Scripture is sufficient to thoroughly equip all Christian

---

19   Towner, *Letters*, 589.
20   See Daniel B. Wallace, *Greek Grammar beyond the Basics: An Exegetical Syntax of the New Testament* (Grand Rapids, MI: Zondervan, 1996), 313–14.
21   Knight, *Pastoral Epistles*, 447.
22   Mounce, *Pastoral Epistles*, 566.

believers so they might please God,[23] and without Scripture they are *un*prepared and *ill*-equipped. Scripture is both necessary and sufficient.

Finally, Timothy is to *continue* in what he has learned and believed (3:14). Negatively, he's not to swerve from or oppose the truth (2:18; 3:8, 13). Positively, he is to guard and entrust to others what he's heard from Paul (1:14; 2:2) and ensure he's fully prepared for ministry through ongoing diligent study and use of the Scriptures, as is fitting for God's worker (2:15). And he is to "preach the word" (*logos*, 4:2), the apostolic message and God's ancient and apostolic written word (4:2 with 3:16).[24]

The Use of Scripture

Paul's own use of Scripture in the letter demonstrates these same convictions about God's written word[25]—chiefly, that what Scripture says, God says; and so it is authoritative and good and speaks with one voice, so there is continuity between the Old Testament and the apostolic gospel, and God's old and new covenant people. Paul's use of the Old Testament is most apparent in two paired citations (2:19), two messianic psalms (3:11; 4:16–18), and the mention of Jesus Christ as "the seed of David" (2:8).

2 Timothy 2:19

Paul wants to reassure Timothy that God's purposes for his people will prevail, despite the apparent success of the opponents, and so he uses God's word from earlier times in salvation history to stress that God's firm foundation, the church, will stand. In the first instance the texts applied to Israel, but now they apply to God's elect in Christ. The two citations (2:19a citing Num. 16:5 LXX; and 2:19b citing Num. 16:26–27 LXX; Isa. 26:13 LXX)[26] function as God's "seal" marking the church, and those in it, as authentically his property.

---

23 Mounce, *Pastoral Epistles*, 571.

24 Mounce, *Pastoral Epistles*, 572–73.

25 B. Paul Wolfe, "The Sagacious Use of Scripture," in *EWTG* 199.

26 See Philip H. Towner, "1–2 Timothy and Titus," in *Commentary on the New Testament Use of the Old Testament*, ed. G. K. Beale and D. A. Carson (Grand Rapids, MI: Baker Academic, 2007), 905–6.

2 Timothy 3:11

Paul calls Timothy to follow him in suffering for the gospel. The apostle does this both by presenting his own persecution and suffering as a model, and by pointing to God's faithful rescue of him. His words evoke Psalm 34:17 and 19 (Ps. 33:18, 20 LXX), where David testifies to the many afflictions of the righteous and the Lord's rescue from them all.[27]

2 Timothy 4:16–18

This important theme of Paul's suffering and impending death for the gospel and the elect reaches a climax in the description of his abandonment and trial. At one level, it's a historical account. But at many points Paul makes use of Psalm 22, a "righteous sufferer" psalm of David fulfilled in Christ's own abandonment, false accusation, trial, crucifixion, and final vindication, and the inclusion of the nations in God's salvation plan (e.g., Mark 15:24, 29, 34, 39). Thus, Christ's experience provides a template for Paul's suffering as a divinely appointed agent of the gospel for the Gentiles.[28] And, as the presence and help of the Lord runs through the psalm, Paul knows the presence and strength of the vindicated, risen Lord Jesus (Col. 1:24) and is assured of his rescue and vindication, even from the lion's mouth (cf. Ps. 22:21). This psalm then functions as a lens for understanding Paul's life and ministry, and can speak truthfully to others, like Timothy, who would also suffer for the gospel.[29]

2 Timothy 2:8

Paul's reference to "the offspring of David" (lit. "seed," *sperma*) is not a Scripture citation, nor is Jesus's *Davidic* kingship a major theme in the letter. Nevertheless, it demonstrates that Paul's use of the Old Testament operated at several levels. It shows that he accepted the historicity of the Davidic account (cf. John 7:42; Rom. 1:3). It reflects Paul's theologi-

---

27 Towner, "Timothy and Titus," 907–8.
28 See Towner, "Timothy and Titus," 909–12.
29 Kuruvilla, *Timothy, Titus*, 193n32.

cal conviction that the gospel is grounded in history.[30] It places Jesus within the unfolding salvation-historical arc of God's purposes and identifies him as the promised eternal King and Savior from David's line (e.g., 2 Sam. 7:16; Jer. 23:5),[31] thus recognizing the continuity of God's plan and his faithfulness in fulfilling his promises in Scripture.[32] As such, despite its brevity, it would have held historical, messianic, eschatological, and pastoral significance for Timothy.

Further Uses

Paul makes use of further Old Testament themes in the Moses-Joshua pattern of his relationship with Timothy (2 Tim. 1:6; 2:1, 24; cf. Num. 27:18–23; Deut. 31:6–7);[33] in Paul's self-understanding of his mission as fulfilling the Abrahamic promise to bless all the nations (2 Tim. 4:17; cf. Gen. 12:3);[34] and in the use of Jewish traditions associated with the biblical account of Moses and the Egyptian magicians as archetypal opponents of God's truth (2 Tim. 3:8; cf. Ex. 7–9).[35]

The Life of God's Word

Second Timothy testifies that there is one God, whose word comes in different forms and from different epochs of salvation history, all of which find their fulfillment in Christ (cf. 2 Cor. 1:20). Paul's presentation of that word is Trinitarian: it is the word of *God* (2 Tim. 2:9, 19; 3:16), about *Christ* (1:8; 2:8), which is guarded by the *Holy Spirit* (1:14). To hear God's word is to hear God. It bears his character and is empowered by him. It is no mere instrument; it is living and active, powerful and free, and it cannot be stopped or hindered (2:9; 3:16; cf. Heb. 4:12). It is a living word that brings life.

God's word advances through human agents. The letter names at least eighteen women and men who partner in the ministry of the word in

30 Yarbrough, *Letters*, 377.
31 Knight, *Pastoral Epistles*, 397.
32 Gordon D. Fee, *1 and 2 Timothy, Titus*, NIBC (Peabody, MA: Hendrickson, 1988), 246.
33 Köstenberger, *Timothy and Titus*, 401–2.
34 Köstenberger, *Timothy and Titus*, 528.
35 Towner, "Timothy and Titus," 906–7.

some way (2 Tim. 1:1–2, 5, 16; 4:10–12, 19–20). Their doctrine and lives align with God's word (1:5; 3:10, 14–15). The false teachers' lives and message, by contrast, do the devil's work (2:16–18, 26; 3:2–5, 13).

Paul's concern is that God's saving mission continues to advance. Even imprisoned, the apostle is undeterred in his ministry (*diakonia*, 4:11; cf. Acts 28). This letter is the fruit of that! Timothy too is to devote himself to the ministry of God's word, to remain in what he has learned and believed (2 Tim. 3:14) and do his best to present himself to God as a worker with no reason to be ashamed for the way he handles God's word (2:15). He can be confident in the future of God's word to save God's elect for eternal glory.

9

Suffering and the Gospel

PAUL WROTE 2 TIMOTHY TO ENSURE the future of the gospel; and, after false teaching, suffering is the next great threat to realizing that goal. It poses a powerful disincentive to gospel faithfulness and ministry. But the reality of suffering looms large in this letter. Paul's life is one of hardship and suffering, and he acknowledges its personal pain and cost. Yet he does not write so that his beloved child will *avoid* suffering. Rather, he wants Timothy to *join* him in suffering and, like him, to fix his eyes on the future horizon of Christ's return, when those who have trusted in Christ will be vindicated and receive their reward.

The Contours of Suffering

Paul's suffering is multidimensional. He has been abandoned and rejected by friends and colleagues (1:15; 4:9–11, 16). He is imprisoned and has lost freedom and comfort (1:16–18; 2:9–10; 4:16–18). He is apart from those he loves (1:4, 17). He is on trial in an unjust "justice" system—notwithstanding his clear conscience (1:3)—and speaks alone in his defense (4:16). He has been persecuted, even stoned, dragged outside a city, and left for dead (3:11; cf. Acts 13:49–52; 14:4–6, 19–22). He anticipates violent execution (2 Tim. 4:6). His enemies actively seek his harm (4:14). He endures cultural shame (1:8, 12). In short, his suffering involves physical deprivation and injury, emotional and existential distress, and loss of reputation, treasured relationships, freedom, and (soon) mortal life itself.

As with God's servants before him—his ancestors (1:3)[1]—Paul's life of faith is marked by trials, hardship, and opposition (e.g., Ex. 1; Pss. 22; 34; 69; Dan. 6).[2] And like them, he patiently endures evil (2 Tim. 2:9, 24; 3:11). The alternative is to give way to cowardice and seek to avoid suffering (1:7), to be ashamed of suffering and those who bear it (1:8), to spiritualize the resurrection and seek to have your best life now (2:18), and to turn from Christ and the gospel in apostasy and false teaching (2:12–13; 3:8; 4:3–4; cf. 2:18).

Reasons for Suffering

In 1 Timothy we glimpse the general suffering of life in this fallen world: Timothy himself has ongoing health issues; some are under the yoke of slavery; and women, even young women, have been widowed, and their welfare is at risk (1 Tim. 5:4–16, 23; 6:1; cf. Rom. 8:19–22). By contrast, the suffering in view in 2 Timothy[3]—and it is a significant theme—is closely related to Christ and the gospel.

Paul is the Lord's prisoner for the gospel (1:8). He has been appointed preacher, apostle, and teacher for the gospel, which is why he suffers (1:12; cf. 3:11). He suffers as "a good soldier of Christ" (2:3). He is in chains because of the gospel (2:9) and endures everything for the elect (2:10). He is willingly "being poured out as a drink offering" (4:6; cf. Num. 28:7), as "a sacrifice for the gospel,"[4] and his death as a martyr is near (2 Tim. 4:6; cf. Phil. 1:23). He has been deserted by Demas, who loves this world more than Christ, and he has suffered from Alexander, who "strongly opposed" the gospel (2 Tim. 4:10, 14–15). Even while he is on trial for his life, Paul's main goal is reaching the nations with the gospel (4:16–17). In short, his apostleship and suffering are intrinsically linked (2 Cor. 11:23–29; Phil. 1:30; Col. 1:24).

---

1   I. Howard Marshall, *The Pastoral Epistles*, ICC (Edinburgh: T&T Clark, 1999), 690.

2   See George Wieland, *The Significance of Salvation: A Study of Salvation Language in the Pastoral Epistles*, PBM (Milton Keynes, UK: Paternoster, 2006), 143–44.

3   There is passing reference to Trophimus's illness (4:19).

4   Philip H. Towner, *The Letters to Timothy and Titus*, NICNT (Grand Rapids, MI: Eerdmans, 2006), 609.

Timothy is to join both Christ and Paul in suffering for the gospel (2 Tim. 1:8; 4:5),[5] even publicly identifying with Paul (and his crucified Lord) by visiting Paul in prison (4:9, 21). Timothy, too, is to suffer as a soldier of Christ (2:3) and, as the Lord's servant, patiently endure evil and correct his opponents with gentleness (2:24–25).

The experience of Paul and Timothy, however, is not unusual. Everyone who lives a godly (*eusebōs*) life in Christ Jesus, who has died with Christ and endured in faith, will be persecuted (2:11–12; 3:12; cf. Rom. 8:17; Phil. 1:29–30). Not all believers will die a martyr's death, as Paul does, but all Christians "*will suffer* as a result of identifying themselves with Christ."[6] This fallen world has rejected God and his Son, and those who follow Christ will, like him, be hated, suffer, and be rejected (John 15:18–21). Believers are not to seek out suffering and shame, but there can be no fair-weather Christians.

Models of Suffering

Given the focus on suffering and the link between suffering and authentic faith and gospel ministry, it is perhaps surprising that Christ's own suffering and death don't feature more prominently in 2 Timothy. Instead, as we have observed, the emphasis falls on Christ's vindication and victory over death rather than his actual suffering and death (1:8; 2:8–12).[7]

The chief model of suffering is Paul. He is the model of faith, life, teaching, and endurance in suffering that Timothy is to follow (3:10–11).[8] He suffers for Christ and the gospel, as Timothy is to do (1:8; 2:3).[9] He is not ashamed of Christ or the gospel, as Timothy is not to be ashamed of Christ, his chained apostle, or the gospel (1:8). Paul has

---

5   Gerald L. Bray, *The Pastoral Epistles*, ITC (London: T&T Clark, 2019), 328.
6   Scott J. Hafemann, "Suffering," in *DPL* 920, italics original.
7   Andreas J. Köstenberger, *Commentary on 1–2 Timothy and Titus*, BTCP (Nashville: Holman Reference, 2017), 372–73.
8   William D. Mounce, *Pastoral Epistles*, WBC 46 (Nashville: Thomas Nelson, 2000), 556–57.
9   In both texts, Paul uses a *syn-* prefix to stress this fellowship in suffering (*synkakopatheō*); BDAG 951.

exemplified to Timothy what he describes in several everyday pictures of exertion and perseverance: a dedicated soldier of Christ, an athlete who has finished the race and won the prize (cf. 1 Cor. 9:24–27), and a hard-working farmer anticipating an eternal reward for his labors (2 Tim. 2:4–6; 4:7–8; cf. 1 Cor. 9:7, 10).[10] As a son follows his father (2 Tim. 1:2; 2:1), Timothy is to give all for Christ and the gospel. So, too, all believers (4:8).

Paul himself follows a pattern. He links to two Davidic psalms that give personal accounts of unjust suffering and God's subsequent vindication and deliverance (2 Tim. 3:11 [Ps. 34:17, 19]; 2 Tim. 4:17 [Ps. 22]).[11] Paul is like David, a righteous sufferer—abandoned by friends and falsely accused—whom the Lord rescued out of all his troubles. These psalms, however, do not just invoke David; they invoke Jesus, *the suffering servant*, who was betrayed, abandoned, and placed on trial, and who prayed for deliverance and mercy. In fact, Psalm 22 is on Jesus's lips as he dies—"My God, my God, why have you forsaken me?" (Matt. 27:46; Mark 15:34; cf. Ps. 22:1)—and is woven through the Gospel accounts of his passion.[12] Paul understands that as David and (especially) Christ trusted in God and God delivered them, so Paul will trust in God, confident that he will be eternally vindicated and delivered, even if he should lose his mortal life (2 Tim. 4:18; cf. 1:12; Isa. 52:13–53:12; 1 Pet. 2:21).

And Paul is not alone! He names men and women from all walks of life who also serve as models: Onesiphorus and his household supported Paul and visited him in prison (2 Tim. 1:16–18; 4:19), as Timothy is now to do (4:9, 21); coworkers continued to partner with Paul (4:10–13, 19–21); and Timothy's own mother and grandmother persevered in faith (1:5). The faithful endurance of all these believers

---

10 Bray, *Pastoral Epistles*, 446.

11 See Philip H. Towner, "1–2 Timothy and Titus," in *Commentary on the New Testament Use of the Old Testament*, ed. G. K. Beale and D. A. Carson (Grand Rapids, MI: Baker Academic, 2007), 907–12; Abraham Kuruvilla, *1 & 2 Timothy, Titus: A Theological Commentary for Preachers* (Eugene, OR: Cascade, 2021), 193.

12 See, for example, David Allen, *According to the Scriptures: The Death of Christ in the Old Testament and the New* (London: SCM, 2018), 44–50, 56–57.

testifies to the gift and sufficiency of God's Spirit to produce power, love, and self-control, not fear (1:7, 14; cf. 2:12).

The End of Suffering

Paul's approach to suffering, however, is not simply to endure it for its own sake. His tone is not one of resignation, despair, or defeat. He knows that Christian suffering has divinely given meaning, purpose, limits, and hope.

First, Christian suffering is a feature of the time between Christ's appearings, when God's salvation has been inaugurated but awaits consummation, and when evil and rebellious people reject and oppose God and his gospel (3:2–4) and persecute his people (3:12). Christian suffering marks this as the eschatological "last days" (3:1; cf. 3:13; 4:3) before Christ's appearing (4:1, 8), when such suffering will end.[13]

Second, Christian suffering is testimony to God's work in a believer's life, as those with an outside show of religion without the Spirit's transforming power to produce a godly life will not be targets of persecution (3:5, 12). As William Mounce observes, "The absence of suffering is a sign that there is something wrong in a believer's life."[14]

Third, suffering and persecution have limited effects. They are temporary. The Lord has rescued Paul before (3:11) and may do so again, but either way, ultimately the Lord will save Paul, and all those who believe in Christ, into his eternal kingdom (2:10; 4:18; cf. Dan. 3:16–18). Suffering and persecution might kill the body, but they cannot kill the soul (2 Tim. 2:12; 4:6–8; cf. Matt. 10:28). The "promise of life" in the gospel is of life and immortality, and all those who believe the gospel will live forever with Christ in glory (2 Tim. 1:10; 2:10–11). Resurrection life remains in the future (2:18), and that future promise far outweighs all present suffering (2 Cor. 4:16–18).

Fourth, suffering gives way to glory, and there is no glory without suffering (Rom. 8:18). It was this way for *Christ* (2 Tim. 1:8–9; 2:8, 10;

---

13 George W. Knight, *Commentary on the Pastoral Epistles*, NIGTC (Grand Rapids, MI: Eerdmans, 1992), 429.

14 Mounce, *Pastoral Epistles*, 584.

4:1, 18; cf. Phil. 2:5–11; Heb. 2:6–10; 12:2). His followers share the same suffering-glory trajectory. We are to die with him and endure suffering and persecution, so to live and reign with him (2 Tim. 1:8; 2:9, 11–12; 3:12; 4:6–8; cf. Matt. 5:10).[15]

Fifth, there will be a future reckoning when Christ appears as righteous Judge (2 Tim. 1:18; 4:1, 8). No person, living or dead, and no deed, good or evil, will escape his judgment (1:18; 2:15; 4:14; cf. 1 Thess. 4:13–17; 2 Thess. 1:6–10). All those who trust in Christ will receive mercy, eternal life, and reward. But he will disown those who deny him or are faithless (2 Tim. 2:12–13; cf. Rom. 11:22).[16] Their only hope is that God may grant them repentance in this life.

Sixth, those who believe and preach the gospel embody the weakness and foolishness of the gospel. This is the way of the cross (1 Cor. 1:17–31). Hence, Paul is not ashamed of the gospel, because he knows it to be the power of God for the salvation of both Jew and Gentile (2 Tim. 1:8–12; cf. Rom. 1:16). The apparent weakness, suffering, and shame of Paul as a minister of the gospel belong to that same divine economy (2 Tim. 2:8–10; cf. 2 Cor. 1:5–7).[17]

Seventh, Paul's suffering is a necessary part of his apostleship and the gospel going to the Gentiles (Acts 9:15–16; 2 Cor. 4:7–12).[18] He suffers and endures everything "for the sake of the elect" (2 Tim. 2:10), and even on trial for his life, he is most concerned that the gospel is "fully proclaimed" among the nations (4:17).

The Suffering of the Gospel

Paul's presentation of suffering is multilayered. It is autobiographical, authentic, hopeful, exhortatory, exemplary, and inspiring. Ultimately, though, it is not about Paul. Everything tracks back to *Christ and the gospel*. Paul suffers as an apostle of Christ and for Christ; and he suffers

---

15 Robert W. Yarbrough, *The Letters to Timothy and Titus*, PNTC (Grand Rapids, MI: Eerdmans, 2018), 380–81.

16 Yarbrough, *Letters*, 382–83.

17 Hafemann, "Suffering," 919.

18 Chiao Ek Ho, "Mission in the Pastoral Epistles," in *EWTG* 259.

because of and for the sake of the gospel and God's elect. Empowered by the Spirit, Timothy is to do the same (1:7). In fact, all believers will suffer persecution for their godly lives in Christ Jesus.

God has set the timetable for history, and at the appointed time, Christ will reappear as Judge. Everyone who endures and longs for that Day will receive the glorious suffering-free resurrection life of his heavenly kingdom. But first they must hear and believe the good news of the Christ who suffered, who was raised to life, and who abolished death and brought to light life and immortality. Truly, without Christ's suffering, there can be no end to suffering.

PART 3

TITUS

God Our Savior

10

The God of Grace

THE CHURCH ON CRETE IS IN ITS INFANCY and Paul is concerned to promote the growth in faith and godliness of God's elect and the progress of the gospel. To this end, he has left Titus there to complete what remains undone, and to appoint church leaders in the many towns across the island (1:5). This letter is further instruction for Titus in that task.

At one level, it's easy to spot similarities between this letter and Paul's letters to Timothy, especially 1 Timothy. They include eligibility criteria for church leaders, instructions for different groups, and instructions for the ministry of Paul's delegate. There are common elements in the presentation of God and salvation, such as the title "Savior," the "then but now" time schema and related "epiphany" theme, and distinctive ethical terms. But as we might expect, given the differences in location, the (im)maturity of the church, the nature of opposition, and the different recipient(s) (Titus 1:4; 3:15), these elements are put to different use. That is, the overlap with the letters to Timothy does not mean their messages are the same or even that the shared features are used in the same way. Each letter must be read on its own terms so that the distinctive messages can be heard.

We don't know the extent of Paul's connection with Crete (Acts 27:7–8, 12),[1] but he is sufficiently familiar with Cretan culture and the

---

1 See William D. Mounce, *Pastoral Epistles*, WBC 46 (Nashville: Thomas Nelson, 2000), 386.

needs of the infant church to know the opportunities and challenges both present to gospel growth and faithfulness. In fact, Paul engages directly with Cretan culture (Titus 1:12–13)[2] and uses his presentation of God and his saving work to provide a sharp contrast with it (cf. Acts 17:22–31).[3]

Another difference between the letters concerns how God's presence is acknowledged. All three letters to Timothy and Titus open and close by invoking divine blessings from God the Father and Christ Jesus (1 Tim. 1:2; 6:21; 2 Tim. 1:2; 4:22a; Titus 1:4; 3:15), but unlike the letters to Timothy, in Titus there are no doxologies, thanksgivings, or prayers (cf. 1 Tim. 1:12, 17; 6:15–16; 2 Tim. 1:3, 18; 4:18, 22b). The result is that God is mentioned *in* the text but not addressed *by* the text. Similarly, the immediacy of God is not as prominent: the "before God (and Christ Jesus)" formula is not found (cf. 1 Tim. 2:3; 5:4, 21; 6:13; 2 Tim. 2:14; 4:1), and although Paul's divine apostolic appointment is mentioned, there are no promises or accounts of God's presence and help (as, e.g., in 1 Tim. 1:12–14; 2 Tim. 2:1, 7; 4:17).

That said, Titus is primarily about God and his salvation: God in his triunity is the main actor,[4] and a "preponderance of God-language" shows "God" (*theos*) to be the most used noun and twenty-eight occurrences of divine names or terms in a letter of only 659 words in the original language (4.25 percent)![5]

---

2   See Andreas J. Köstenberger, *Commentary on 1–2 Timothy and Titus*, BTCP (Nashville: Holman Reference, 2017), 301–2; Philip H. Towner, *The Letters to Timothy and Titus*, NICNT (Grand Rapids, MI: Eerdmans, 2006), 64, 74; Reggie M. Kidd, "Titus as *Apologia*: Grace for Liars, Beasts, and Bellies," *HBT* 21 (1999): 207.

3   See Riemer Faber, " 'Evil Beasts, Lazy Gluttons': A Neglected Theme in the Epistle to Titus," *WTJ* 67 (2005): 135–45; George M. Wieland, "Roman Crete and the Letter to Titus," *NTS* 55 (2009): 338–54; Luke Timothy Johnson, "The Pedagogy of Grace: The Experiential Basis of Morality in Titus," in *REGW* 38–51.

4   As the subject of active verbs (1:2–3; 2:11, 14 [3x]; 3:5–6) and agent of passive verbs (1:3; 3:4).

5   I have added the one mention of the Holy Spirit to Yarbrough's tally: God (*theos*, 13x), Jesus (*Iēsous*, 4x), Christ (*Christos*, 4x), Holy Spirit (*pneuma hagion*, 1x), and Savior (*sōtēr*, 6x). Robert W. Yarbrough, *The Letters to Timothy and Titus*, PNTC (Grand Rapids, MI: Eerdmans, 2018), 13–14.

It is as if Titus (and the Cretan believers) needed apostolic directions, but not the personal encouragement and entreaty that Paul thought Timothy (and the Ephesians) needed. The letter to Titus is short, to the point, and almost businesslike. And yet, the three dense statements about God and his salvation plan are so essential to the instructions (1:1–4; 2:11–14; 3:4–7) that, notwithstanding the practical nature of the letter, without these its message would be entirely different.

The God Who Never Lies

God's role in salvation dominates the presentation of God. He is the initiator, source, and author of his plan to save.[6] Unlike the varied titles for divinity in 1 and 2 Timothy, "Savior" (*sōtēr*) is the only title used for God besides "Father." Paul uses the title in relation to God's saving intervention in the Christ event (Titus 3:4) and God's command to Paul regarding the proclamation of God's word of promise (1:3), and to describe the sum total of Christian teaching as being "about God our Savior" (2:10).[7]

In fact, "Savior" appears in Titus more than in any other New Testament writing. But whereas "Savior" is used of God alone in 1 Timothy and of Christ alone in 2 Timothy, here both God the Father[8] and Jesus Christ (Titus 1:4; 2:13; 3:6) are named "our Savior" three times each and in close proximity, reflecting an "easy interchange"[9] and/or convergence in the activities of God and Christ in salvation. Moreover, whereas 1 Timothy focuses on God's *desire* to save all people, and 2 Timothy on God's *power* to save, in Titus the focus is on God's *character*, which guarantees his salvation: he is the God who never lies.

This description might not strike us as unusual. After all, the truthfulness and reliability of God and his word are consistent themes throughout Scripture (e.g., Num. 23:19; Ps. 89:35; Heb. 6:18) and

---

6   Chiao Ek Ho, "Mission in the Pastoral Epistles," in *EWTG* 244.

7   Towner, *Letters*, 739.

8   George W. Knight, *Commentary on the Pastoral Epistles*, NIGTC (Grand Rapids, MI: Eerdmans, 1992), 315.

9   Gordon D. Fee, *Pauline Christology: An Exegetical-Theological Study* (Peabody, MA: Hendrickson, 2007), 438.

guarantee his covenant with his people and his promises of both salvation and judgment. The people of Crete, though, were known to be
liars (Titus 1:12), to the extent that terms for lying even made use of
the word "Crete": to speak like a Cretan was to lie![10] The chief reason
for their reputation was their claim to possess the tomb of Zeus, their
great god, when it was widely held that gods did not die.[11] But Zeus
himself was also notorious for lies and trickery.[12] Of course, Paul wasn't
buying into any of that. He knew that Zeus was no god at all (cf. 1 Cor.
8:4; Gal. 4:8), but his mention of the Cretans as liars likely also alluded
to their lying god. In effect, Paul was drawing a sharp contrast: the gods
and people of Crete lie, but the true God does not![13]

God's word is true, *and* he is true to his word—always and entirely.
Unlike the opponents (Titus 1:16), there is no gap between God's word
and his deeds. He promised eternal life for his elect (1 Tim. 4:8; 2 Tim.
1:1) before time began, and now, at his own right time, he has revealed
(*phaneroō*) and is fulfilling that promise through the proclamation
(*kērygma*) of his word (*logos*, i.e., the gospel and related teaching),
which he entrusted to his servant Paul by his command (Titus 1:1–3).
The timeline of history maps the progressive revelation and implementation of God's previously hidden salvation plan (1:3; 2:11, 13; 3:4),
which in the present era is to be carried forward by Paul's proclamation, and that of Titus and others (1:9; 2:1, 8,[14] 15; cf. 1:4; 2:7; 3:1–2).
By contrast, the deceptive teaching of the opponents was destroying
faith, households, and the believing community. *Their* words must be
silenced (1:11, 14; 3:9–10).

God's gospel word is trustworthy and true (*pistos*, 1:9; 3:8; cf. 3:4–7)[15]
and produces saving faith and knowledge of the truth in his people
(1:1, 13–14; 3:8). In fact, the connection between God and his word

---

10   E.g., LSJ, *krētizō*, s.v. 995; Wieland, "Roman Crete," 345.

11   Faber, "Evil Beasts," 136.

12   Wieland, "Roman Crete," 346.

13   Kidd, "Titus as *Apologia*," 198.

14   "Sound speech" (*logon hygiē*) could refer to Titus's speech generally but more likely de-
     scribes the content of his teaching. Towner, *Letters*, 732, suggests "the authorized gospel."

15   I. Howard Marshall, *The Pastoral Epistles*, ICC (Edinburgh: T&T Clark, 1999), 167.

and his mission is such that believers, even those of low social status in the culture of the day, can bring dishonor or adornment not to God's *name*, as we might have expected (Isa. 52:5; Ezek. 36:20–23; Rom. 2:24), but to God's *message* (Titus 2:5, 10; cf. 1 Tim. 6:1), and thereby hinder or serve his mission.

God's character is further displayed in salvation. He is a God of relationships, benevolence, and love. He chose his "elect" (Titus 1:1; cf. 1 Chron. 16:13; Isa. 42:1; Rom. 8:33; 2 Tim. 1:9) and acted in salvation entirely because of his grace (*charis*) and mercy (*eleos*), not the merit of our deeds (Titus 2:11; 3:5, 7; cf. Deut. 9:4–6). He saved "us." He justifies us. He makes us heirs of eternal life (Titus 3:7). He pours out the Holy Spirit upon us generously (3:5–6). So much is his character displayed in salvation that Paul personifies divine attributes as actors in redemption:[16] "*the grace of God* has appeared" bringing salvation and training us (2:11); and "when *the goodness and loving kindness of God* our Savior appeared, he saved us" (3:4–5; cf. Rom. 2:4; 1 Cor. 1:30).

Unbelievers, and especially the opponents, are characterized by evil, greed, empty talk, and troublemaking (Titus 1:11–16; 3:3, 9–11), but God is characterized by peace, grace, mercy, kindness, and love (1:4; 2:11; 3:5, 7), *and* he is not capricious, as Zeus was said to be. The constancy of God's desire to save, from before the ages began and into the eternal future, and his absolute power to achieve that salvation are on open display in the Christ event and its related gospel proclamation (1:2; 3:7; cf. 1 Tim. 2:4; 2 Tim. 1:8–9), and in the faith and godly lives of his elect (Titus 2:7). God's word is certain, and his salvation is sure.

Intertwined with this central theme of his provision of salvation is God's role as teacher.[17] We see this at several points. His educative interventions create and define the different epochs of history, and his educative saving grace is *the* defining feature of this present age (1:3; 2:11–12; 3:4).[18] He is both the teacher and the content of instruction.

16 Greg A. Couser, "The Sovereign Savior of 1 and 2 Timothy and Titus," in *EWTG* 134n125.
17 See Claire S. Smith, "Ethics of Teaching and Learning in Christianity Today: Insights from the Book of Titus," in *REGW* 237–54.
18 Smith, "Ethics," 243, 249.

His saving intervention teaches (*paideuō*, 2:12) and transforms those who were ignorant of God,[19] disobedient to him,[20] and deceived (3:3), now giving them knowledge of the (his) truth and a common faith (1:1, 4). His appointed workers have educational mandates (Paul: 1:1, 3; overseers: 1:9; Titus: 2:1, 7, 15; 3:1; cf. older women: 2:3; cf. 3:14) and teach recognized content (*didachē*) that is trustworthy (*pistos*, 1:9; 3:8) and healthy/sound (*hygiainō*, 1:9; 2:1, 8; cf. 2:7, 15; 3:1–2; 2 Tim. 1:13). His educational enterprise differs from that of the opponents in origin, purpose, truth, content, manner, method, and outcome. For those who learn (Titus 3:14), it is a difference between eternal life and (self-)condemnation (3:11; 1:16; cf. Matt. 12:37).[21]

Christ, the Exalted Savior

Salvation also dominates the presentation of Christ. In fact, the correlation/coordination or "easy interchange"[22] of God the Father and Jesus Christ in salvation is a feature of Titus. Both are "our Savior" (God: 1:3; 2:10; 3:4; Christ: 1:4; 2:13; 3:6); both have an elect people (1:1; 2:14); both advance the soteriological project through "appearings" (2:11, 13; 3:4; cf. 1:3); both are the source and givers of the salvation blessings of grace and peace (1:4; 2:13; 3:6); and both commission Paul's apostolic proclamation (1:1, 3). But the overlap is not restricted to function: Jesus Christ is also called *God*.

This claim hangs on the translation of 2:13, which poses perhaps *the* interpretative crux of the letter. Part of the difficulty, as George Wieland puts it, is that the verse contains a "cascade of ideas . . . [exhibiting] more impressionistic artistry than grammatical exactitude," so it is difficult to know how the ideas relate to each other.[23] It is clear that believers are waiting for an eschatological "appearing," but who or what will appear? Three options present themselves: "the glory

---

19   Marshall, *Pastoral Epistles*, 309.

20   Mounce, *Pastoral Epistles*, 446.

21   Mounce, *Pastoral Epistles*, 455.

22   Fee, *Pauline Christology*, 438.

23   George Wieland, *The Significance of Salvation: A Study of Salvation Language in the Pastoral Epistles*, PBM (Milton Keynes, UK: Paternoster, 2006), 206.

of our great God *and* of our Savior Jesus Christ";[24] "the *glory* of our great God and Savior, [which is] Jesus Christ";[25] and "the glory of *our great God and Savior Jesus Christ.*" On linguistic, grammatical, and theological grounds, the third option is the most likely, meaning that Jesus Christ is called "God" (John 1:1, 18; 20:28; Rom. 9:5).[26] In a similar vein, the only two terms used for the Father, "God" and "Savior," are also the only two titles applied to Christ Jesus, signaling and highlighting their shared divine status and equal contribution to salvation. Notably, "Lord," used of both the Father and Christ to similar effect in 2 Timothy, is not used at all. Titus is the only one of Paul's letters not to use the title.

Thus, notwithstanding the "scarcity of references"[27] to Christ (Titus 1:4; 2:13–14; 3:6), Titus presents a high Christology. In the culture of Crete, this might have had a polemical edge, as Zeus was believed to have received divine status only in response to his benefaction toward people.[28] It also defied the emperor cult.[29] More generally, though, the effect of this high Christology is to show that every aspect of salvation has been secured by a *divine* Savior.

First Timothy stressed Christ's shared humanity with and mediatorial role for all people, and 2 Timothy highlighted his vindication and exaltation following suffering and humiliation. But here in Titus he is the "great" (*megas*) Savior God, the embodied manifestation of God's grace, goodness, and loving-kindness, who appeared (*epiphainō*, 2:11; 3:4) in history *from above* to give himself for those he saves. As Yahweh did for Israel under the old covenant, Christ, through his atoning death, redeemed and purified a people for his own possession (2:14;

24 So, J. N. D. Kelly, *The Pastoral Epistles: I & II Timothy, Titus* (London: Black, 1963), 246.

25 So, Towner, *Letters*, 754.

26 See Murray J. Harris, *Jesus as God: The New Testament Use of Theos in Reference to Jesus* (Grand Rapids, MI: Baker, 1992), 178–85; Mounce, *Pastoral Epistles*, 425–31; Knight, *Pastoral Epistles*, 322–26; John Stott, *The Message of 1 Timothy and Titus*, BST (London: Inter-Varsity Press, 1996), 188–89; Wieland, *Significance*, 207.

27 Daniel L. Akin, "The Mystery of Godliness Is Great: Christology in the Pastoral Epistles," in *EWTG* 142.

28 Towner, *Letters*, 64, 740–42.

29 Köstenberger, *Timothy and Titus*, 339.

cf. Ex. 19:5; Deut. 7:6; 14:2; Ezek. 37:23).[30] And the future appearing (*epiphaneia*) of his divine glory (*doxa*) is the blessed hope of his people,[31] which will bring this present age to an end (Titus 2:13; cf. Col. 3:4; 2 Thess. 1:9–10).

Holy Spirit

The one brief reference to the Spirit in Titus confirms the thoroughly Trinitarian nature of salvation as it is both accomplished and applied: God our Savior saved us through the washing of regeneration and renewal of the Holy Spirit (*pneuma hagios*), whom he poured out richly on us, through Jesus Christ our Savior (Titus 3:4–6). This creedal statement has a lot to say about salvation, which is the subject of the next chapter, but it also tells us about the Spirit.

The Holy Spirit is the gift of God the Father[32] to those he has saved. He has been *generously poured out* on us (Acts 2:17–18, 33; 10:45). He comes to us from the Father, (only) through Christ (John 14:26; Acts 2:33). In salvation history, this fulfills God's promise that he would pour out his Spirit on all his people—those who now believe in Christ—and designates the present as the "last days" before the Lord comes (Acts 2:17–21, 33; cf. Joel 2:28–32). The Spirit's washing brings salvation, regeneration, and renewal to sinners (Ps. 51:10; Ezek. 36:25–27; Acts 15:7–11; 1 Cor. 6:9–11), cleansing from sin and producing radically changed lives marked by good works that advance God's mission (Titus 2:14).[33] The outpouring of the Spirit on us is also "the evidence that we have been justified by grace" and have been given "the promise of adoption leading to eternal life"[34] (3:7). So, although the title "our Savior" is not applied to the Spirit, his ministry is integral to salvation, and he works in union with God our Savior and Christ our Savior to bring salvation into effect in our hearts and lives. As Mounce observes,

30 Towner, *Letters*, 763.
31 Knight, *Pastoral Epistles*, 322.
32 See Gerald L. Bray, *The Pastoral Epistles*, ITC (London: T&T Clark, 2019), 552.
33 Köstenberger, *Timothy and Titus*, 348.
34 Bray, *Pastoral Epistles*, 552.

"Throughout the process there is a threefold presentation of the God-head, God the Father initiating the process, made possible through the work of the Son and actuated by the Holy Spirit."[35]

———

The two main aspects of the presentation of the triune God in Titus—namely, that God is Savior and God alone possesses moral perfection—tell us about who God is *in himself* and how he is *toward us*, his people. He is the unlying God. He is the source and giver of grace, peace, love, goodness, purity, mercy, hope, and righteousness. He is generous and self-giving. His word is trustworthy and true, and there is no discrepancy between his word and actions, even across the epochs of time.

This is how God, as triune Savior, is toward his people. He elected a people for his own and promised them eternal life; his grace, goodness and loving-kindness have appeared in history in the person and work of Christ to accomplish their redemption; and Christ will appear again to fulfill their eschatological hope of eternal life. Until then, God's people, especially their leaders, are to learn from God to live lives that reflect *his* character, having been cleansed from sin, reborn and renewed and enabled by his Holy Spirit, so we can commend God and his salvation to those among whom we live.

35 Mounce, *Pastoral Epistles*, 455.

11

He Saved Us

THE WORD "GOSPEL" (*EUANGELION*) does not appear in Titus. In fact, it is the only letter of Paul's where this is so. Yet Titus contains at least one of the pithiest, clearest statements about salvation, and about the involvement of the Trinity in salvation, in the entire New Testament (i.e., 3:4–7).[1]

But the letter's teaching on salvation wasn't formulated in a vacuum. The pressing issue on Crete was that, for the sake of shameful financial gain, opponents were teaching what should *not* be taught and disrupting the faith, functioning, and effective godly witness of entire households and individual believers (1:10–16). If God's saving work was to advance, Titus must silence these charlatans, establish sound church leadership (1:5–9, 11, 13; 3:10), and remind all believers of their privilege and duty as God's elect to be aligned with his salvation agenda (e.g., 2:1–10, 15; 3:1–2, 8, 14).

Who Is Saved?

Those who have been saved are "God's elect" (*eklektos theou*, 1:1; cf. Rom. 8:33; Col. 3:12) and "a people" who are Jesus Christ's "own possession" (Titus 2:14). They are repeatedly identified as "us":[2] Jewish

---

1 Gerald L. Bray, *The Pastoral Epistles*, ITC (London: T&T Clark, 2019), 552.
2 The plural, first person pronoun (*hēmas*) appears fifteen times in Titus (1:3, 4; 2:8, 10, 12, 13, 14 [2x]; 3:3, 4, 5 [2x], 6 [2x], 15), and the singular form (*egō*) four times (nineteen in

Paul, Gentile Titus, Cretan believers, and all Christians.[3] They form
a clearly differentiated group within wider society. But that was not
always the case.

They were once like everyone else. They, too, were yet to believe
in God, and without the educating benefit of God's grace and the
renewing and transforming inner work of his Spirit (2:11; 3:5). Like
the unbelieving world (3:3), they were "foolish, disobedient, [and]
led astray" in their knowledge of God—ignorant of him, disobedient
to him (cf. Ex. 23:21 LXX; Deut. 1:26 LXX; Rom. 10:21; 11:30; Titus
1:16), and deceived from the right path.[4] They were enslaved (*douleuō*,
3:3; cf. 2:3) to worldly passions, filled with malice, envy, and hate (Eph.
4:17–23). They were ruled by rebellious "ungodliness" (*asebeia*, Titus
2:12; cf. Rom. 1:18; 11:26)[5] and evil[6] lawlessness (*anomia*, Titus 2:14; cf.
Rom. 4:7; 6:19; 2 Cor. 6:14), from which they needed to be redeemed,
purified, and cleansed.

And Paul does not want Titus and Cretan believers to forget what
they once were (cf. 1 Cor. 6:9–11).[7] If Christians prior to their conversion were at all different from the rest of the Cretan population, with its
well-earned reputation as perpetual "liars, evil beasts, and lazy gluttons"
(Titus 1:12), or from the opponents, who were worse still,[8] it could
only have been a difference of degree, not of kind. It was a problem of
the heart. Those who would come to faith had nothing to commend
themselves before God. Without God, *no one* was saved, even on the

total). This is reversed in 2 Timothy, where singular forms occur thirty-three times, and
plural forms, only nine times (forty-two in total). Cf. George W. Knight, *Commentary on
the Pastoral Epistles*, NIGTC (Grand Rapids, MI: Eerdmans, 1992), 319.

3 Cf. Philip H. Towner, *The Letters to Timothy and Titus*, NICNT (Grand Rapids, MI: Eerdmans, 2006), 781n46.

4 Claire S. Smith, "Ethics of Teaching and Learning in Christianity Today: Insights from
the Book of Titus," in *REGW* 246.

5 Luke Timothy Johnson, *Letters to Paul's Delegates: 1 Timothy, 2 Timothy, Titus*. The New
Testament in Context (Valley Forge, PA: Trinity, 1996), 237.

6 I. Howard Marshall, *The Pastoral Epistles*, ICC (Edinburgh: T&T Clark, 1999), 283, 285.

7 William D. Mounce, *Pastoral Epistles*, WBC 46 (Nashville: Thomas Nelson, 2000), 446.

8 Luke Timothy Johnson, "The Pedagogy of Grace: The Experiential Basis of Morality in
Titus," in *REGW* 42.

basis of their own works of righteousness (*dikaiosynē*, 3:5; cf. Rom. 3:20), whether ethical good deeds, Jewish law observance and purity rules, or pagan ritual. This is why the opponents posed such a threat (Titus 1:10–16). There could be no salvation with them.

God's Plan

Salvation is God's work from beginning to end and an expression of his grace and favor toward undeserving humanity. Humanity is characterized by our hatred of one another (3:3); *he* is characterized by his benevolent love and saving interventions on our behalf. He saved us, not because of *our* works but only because of "*his own* mercy" (*eleos*, 3:5); and he saved us through the manifestation in history of his grace (2:11), and his goodness and loving-kindness (3:4). That is, in his salvation plan we see how God is toward us.

His salvation tracks a course of being once hidden but now revealed, and from promise to fulfillment, as God's plan, known only to him, is made known and accomplished in time and space.[9] At every point, he is its initiator, author, and source. He established his plan and freely chose his elect and promised eternal life before time began (1:1–2; 3:7).[10] He revealed and accomplished salvation in history when his grace and goodness and loving-kindness appeared (*epiphainō*) in the Christ event—Christ's incarnate life, atoning death, resurrection, and ascension. He made known (*phaneroō*) his salvation "in his own time" (NET), through the preaching of his word at his command by his servant Paul and, by extension, those after Paul (1:1, 3; cf. 1:4, 9). And his salvation will be consummated at the eschatological appearing (*epiphaneia*) of Jesus Christ, when the hope of salvation will be fully realized (1:2; 2:13; 3:7). Until then, in "the present [*nyn*] age" (2:12) between Christ's two appearings, salvation is received by faith (1:1; 2:2; 3:8) and demonstrated in godly living (2:12, 14; 3:14).

---

9   See Philip H. Towner, *The Goal of Our Instruction: The Structure of Theology and Ethics in the Pastoral Epistles*, JSNTSup 34 (Sheffield: JSOT, 1989), 61–71.

10 Knight, *Pastoral Epistles*, 284–85.

Salvation comes from God's mercy, grace, goodness, and loving-kindness. His mercy (Ex. 34:6–7; Rom. 9:23; 11:31; 15:9; Eph. 2:4) is his undeserved benevolence to those in need, especially of salvation.[11] His grace (*charis*, Titus 1:4; 2:11; 3:7; cf. Gen. 6:8 LXX; Ex. 33:17 LXX; Eph. 2:8) is his unmerited and unsolicited favor.[12] His goodness (*chrēstotēs*, Titus 3:4) finds expression in his gentleness[13] and forbearance (cf. Pss. 25:7 [24:7 LXX]; 31:19 [30:20 LXX]; 68:10 [67:11 LXX]; Luke 6:35; Rom. 2:4; 11:22; Eph. 2:7), and is coupled with his "love for mankind" (NET; *philanthrōpia*, Titus 3:4).[14] These qualities, except for mercy, were commonly attributed to Greco-Roman gods and rulers, and Paul may be co-opting that cultural frame to portray God as the ideal benevolent ruler.[15] But the Old Testament is the richer and more immediate background, as these qualities of divine grace and mercy (Heb. *hesed*) and goodness characterize Yahweh's covenant relationship with his elect—as they do in Titus.

Christ's Self-Giving

As the manifestation of God's grace and goodness and loving-kindness, Christ is the agent of God's salvation. Like the Father, he is three times called "our Savior" in Titus, but *how* he saves is stated in a single, simple phrase: "who gave himself for us" (*hos edōken heauton hyper hēmōn*, 2:14).

Evoking Jesus's own words about his death (Matt. 20:28; Mark 10:45), Paul identifies Jesus's self-sacrificial death on the cross as the means by which salvation was achieved when Christ died *for us* (Rom. 5:6–8; Gal. 1:4; 2:20; 1 Tim. 2:6). He did this for two purposes: to redeem or ransom[16] (*lytroō*) us from "all lawlessness" (namely, the power and consequences

---

11 Mounce, *Pastoral Epistles*, 11; Knight, *Pastoral Epistles*, 66.

12 John Stott, *The Message of 1 Timothy and Titus*, BST (London: Inter-Varsity Press, 1996), 165.

13 Johnson, "Pedagogy," 48.

14 Knight, *Pastoral Epistles*, 338.

15 Marshall, *Pastoral Epistles*, 134; Abraham Kuruvilla, *1 & 2 Timothy, Titus: A Theological Commentary for Preachers* (Eugene, OR: Cascade, 2021), 225; Andreas J. Köstenberger, *Commentary on 1–2 Timothy and Titus*, BTCP (Nashville: Holman Reference, 2017), 347.

16 See Leon Morris, *The Apostolic Preaching of the Cross* (Grand Rapids, MI: Eerdmans, 1965), 15–16, 38–39.

of evil)[17] and to purify (*katharizō*) for himself a people for his own possession. The price of our redemption was *himself*. And he died *in place
of us*.[18] He is both "priest and victim."[19] The supreme condescension
and humility of this is clear from the preceding verse: the one who gave
himself for us is none other than "our *great God and Savior*" (Titus 2:13).

Linguistic and thematic cues identify his saving work as the fulfillment of key Old Testament events and promises. Christ is "our Passover,
our exodus and our Sinai,"[20] and he fulfills God's exilic promises.

- In the exodus, Yahweh redeemed his people Israel from slavery,
  which became emblematic of God's deliverance (e.g., Ex. 6:6;
  13:3, 14; Pss. 106:10; 107:2; Isa. 41:14; 43:1); they escaped death
  through the death of a substitute. Now Christ redeems God's
  elect from bondage to sin (Titus 2:3; 3:3),[21] having given himself
  in substitutionary death for his people (1 Cor. 5:7).

- At Sinai, the terms of the covenant were that Israel would be to
  Yahweh a people of his own possession (*laos periousios*, LXX: Ex.
  19:5; 23:22; Deut. 7:6). Paul uses the same phrase here for believers
  as Christ's possession (Titus 2:14).[22]

- And during the exile, Yahweh promises to rescue Israel from all
  their lawless deeds, and to cleanse them, and to make them his
  people (Ezek. 37:23; cf. Ps. 130:8 [129:8 LXX]; Ezek. 36:25, 29, 31,
  33);[23] Christ has now done this for believers.

Thus, Paul shows that Yahweh's promises of redemption under the
old covenant have been fulfilled by Christ, and that Christians are

17 Marshall, *Pastoral Epistles*, 283, 285.
18 Knight, *Pastoral Epistles*, 327.
19 Bray, *Pastoral Epistles*, 527.
20 Stott, *Timothy and Titus*, 189.
21 Philip H. Towner, "1–2 Timothy and Titus," in *Commentary on the New Testament Use of
    the Old Testament*, ed. G. K. Beale and D. A. Carson (Grand Rapids, MI: Baker Academic,
    2007), 913.
22 Köstenberger, *Timothy and Titus*, 340.
23 Towner, "Timothy and Titus," 913–15.

the new Israel, chosen and treasured, rescued and redeemed. Redemption is offered no longer to Jews only but to "all people" (Titus 2:11; cf. 1 Tim. 2:4; 4:10): Jews and Gentiles, men and women, slaves and free (Titus 1:1, 4; 2:2–10; cf. Gal. 3:28).

Saved by the Spirit

The redemption secured by Christ is applied to those God has saved through the gift and work of the Holy Spirit, whom God the Father has "poured out on us richly through Jesus Christ our Savior" (Titus 3:6). Since the inception of the church at Pentecost, this has been the experience of all who trust in Christ (Acts 2:17–18, 33). Salvation is not an entirely future experience that awaits the final appearing of Christ; when God saves, he comes to us by his Spirit, whom he lavishes upon us, and effects salvation in us *now*.

Three aspects of the Spirit's work are named: "washing," "regeneration," and "renewal" (Titus 3:5). Their exact interrelationship is much debated,[24] but taken individually, "washing" (*loutron*) is used here not for water baptism[25] but as a metaphor for spiritual cleansing and purifying from sin[26] (cf. 2:14; Eph. 5:26); "regeneration" (*palingenesia*) is rebirth or new birth (cf. John 3:3–8);[27] and "renewal" (*anakainōsis*) is inner transformation (cf. Rom. 12:2). Some interpreters see "regeneration" and "renewal" as synonyms for the one activity.[28] With other

---

24 E.g., George Wieland, *The Significance of Salvation: A Study of Salvation Language in the Pastoral Epistles*, PBM (Milton Keynes, UK: Paternoster, 2006), 224–25, identifies five possible readings.

25 See Mounce, *Pastoral Epistles*, 437–40; Gordon D. Fee, *God's Empowering Presence: The Holy Spirit in the Letters of Paul* (Peabody, MA: Hendrickson, 1994), 780–81; Towner, *Goal*, 116–17.

26 Knight, *Pastoral Epistles*, 342.

27 Robert W. Yarbrough, *The Letters to Timothy and Titus*, PNTC (Grand Rapids, MI: Eerdmans, 2018), 546.

28 E.g., Fee, *Empowering Presence*, 781–82; Michael A. G. Haykin, "The Fading Vision? The Spirit and Freedom in the Pastoral Epistles," *EvQ* 57 (1985): 303; Ben Witherington III, *A Socio-Rhetorical Commentary on Titus, 1–2 Timothy and 1–3 John*, vol. 1 of *Letters and Homilies for Hellenized Christians* (Downers Grove, IL: InterVarsity, 2006), ProQuest Ebook Central, https://ebookcentral.proquest.com/lib/moore/detail.action?docID=2030868), 160.

interpreters,[29] I see them as different aspects of conversion (albeit closely related): "the washing of regeneration" is spiritual rebirth that cleanses us from our past sinful life (Titus 3:3); and "renewal" is spiritual transformation that allows and produces godly living (2:12, 14; 3:1–2). Thus, "conversion consists negatively of a cleansing and positively of a renewal brought about by the Holy Spirit."[30] Either way, the saving work of the Spirit effects these changes (Ezek. 36:25–28). Our transformation from lawlessness is brought about not by the addition of laws but by a change of heart effected by the Spirit.[31] By means of *his* work, we are made new (2 Cor. 5:17).

Salvation Now and Not Yet

God saved us (and poured out his transforming Holy Spirit on us) so that (*hina*),[32] having been justified by his grace, we might become heirs, with the hope of eternal life (Titus 3:7).[33] There are several things to note here. First is the contrast between our futile works of righteousness (*dikaiosynē*, 3:5) and being acquitted and *declared* righteous by God (*dikaiōthentes*).[34] Second, our justification is entirely a gift of grace (*charis*) from God the Father,[35] which believers have already been granted. Third, God saves us so that we might become heirs, which implies our adoption now as his sons/children (Rom. 8:17; Gal. 4:6–7).[36] Fourth, this is associated with the work of the Spirit and justification (Rom. 4:13–14; 8:15–17; 1 Cor. 6:9–11; Gal. 3:11–29; 4:6–7; Eph. 1:13–14).[37] Fifth, as heirs we have a right to an assured future possession,[38] and currently stand in a "privileged and

---

29 See Mounce, *Pastoral Epistles*, 441–43, 448; Kuruvilla, *Timothy, Titus*, 226; Yarbrough, *Letters*, 546.
30 Mounce, *Pastoral Epistles*, 448.
31 Johnson, "Pedagogy," 47, 49.
32 Towner, *Letters*, 786.
33 Knight, *Pastoral Epistles*, 346.
34 Wieland, *Significance*, 232.
35 Mounce, *Pastoral Epistles*, 450.
36 Marshall, *Pastoral Epistles*, 324.
37 Towner, *Letters*, 788.
38 Marshall, *Pastoral Epistles*, 324.

anticipatory position" before God.[39] Sixth, our inheritance is eternal life, promised by God before time began (Titus 1:2). And finally, this means that believers' present experience as heirs is one of "now and not yet," while we await the full receipt of our inheritance when Christ appears (2:13). For now, we hope in our certain future.

From what does God save us? Unlike 1 and 2 Timothy and elsewhere in Paul's letters (e.g., Rom. 14:10; 2 Cor. 5:10; 2 Thess. 1:9; 1 Tim. 5:24; 6:9; 2 Tim. 2:12–13), there are no clear statements about eschatological judgment in Titus. Instead, salvation is cast in terms of rescue and redemption from lawlessness and a morally defiled life lived in rebellion against God and enslaved to worldly passions (e.g., Titus 2:2, 12, 14; 3:1–2). Implicitly, though, believers are also saved from the alternative to eternal life (i.e., death); from not being acquitted by God (i.e., guilt); and from not being God's elect (i.e., exclusion and non-heirs). The stress on sound/healthy faith and teaching (1:9; 2:1–2, 8,[40] 15; 3:8; cf. 1:4; 2:7), the urgent need to silence false teaching and divisive people (1:11, 13; 3:10–11), and especially the fact that God our Savior *commands* that his word be proclaimed (1:3) also betray the gravity of not having saving faith and personal knowledge of the truth (1:16), and therefore not being saved.

———

Salvation in Titus is explicitly and actively the work of all three persons of the Godhead: "Ultimately all saving work is attributed to God the Father, with Christ serving as his agent in both salvation and the giving of the Spirit, and with the Spirit serving as his agent in regeneration."[41] Salvation is not a half measure or equivocal; it has been revealed and accomplished by God in his triunity! As such, it shows God's immense benevolence, grace, and condescension, and his unchanging will (1:2; cf. Num. 23:19) to make a people for his own possession for all eternity.

39 Knight, *Pastoral Epistles*, 347.
40 Towner, *Letters*, 732.
41 Köstenberger, *Timothy and Titus*, 346. His comment is about Titus 3:4–6, but it aptly applies to the letter.

The beneficiaries of salvation are "us"—not, as in 1 Timothy, the indefinite group of those who are to be saved (1:16; 2:4, 6; 4:10; cf. Titus 2:11) but those whom God *has already* saved and regenerated and cleansed and renewed. *We* are his heirs of eternal life—not by any merit of our own but entirely through trust and dependence on the free gift of God.

12

Our People, God's Elect

THOSE WHOM GOD HAS SAVED are a newly constituted people, with a collective identity that operates internally and externally. Internally, they are "our people" (Titus 3:14), who share a common experience of God's saving and educating grace in a community shaped by his word.[1] Externally, they are to stand out from their godless, hostile, and morally bankrupt society, united in the common purpose of advancing God's saving plan.

Those whom God has saved have also been made new individually.[2] This is why they are no longer who they once were (3:3). Their personal faith in God and his salvation—summed up in the "trustworthy" saying—produces godly living (3:8; cf. 1:16). But this new life is no mere external display of virtue. They have been born again and renewed by the Holy Spirit (3:5), so their ethic is not merely "*do* this" but, rather, "*become* who you *are*."

A New Identity

Believers have a new identity. They are "God's elect," chosen by God before the ages began (1:1–2; cf. Col. 3:12; 2 Tim. 1:9; 2:10) and before any choice or contribution of their own (Titus 3:5). They stand

---

1   See Ray Van Neste, " 'Our People': Ethics and the Identity of the People of God in the Letter to Titus," in *REGW* 189–210.

2   George Wieland, *The Significance of Salvation: A Study of Salvation Language in the Pastoral Epistles*, PBM (Milton Keynes, UK: Paternoster, 2006), 222; I. Howard Marshall, *The Pastoral Epistles*, ICC (Edinburgh: T&T Clark, 1999), 305.

in continuity with God's people under the old covenant—loved and chosen by God, called and redeemed to serve him (Deut. 7:6–8; Pss. 105:6, 43; 106:5; Isa. 42:1)—but God's elect are now Jews *and Gentiles*, saved through faith in his promises (Titus 1:1, 4; 2:11; 3:8; cf. Rom. 2:25–29).[3] Like Israel of old, they have obligations of holiness and obedience, and are to be a blessing to the nations (Titus 3:1–2, 8; cf. Gen. 12:3; Jer. 29:7).[4]

They are also "a people of [Christ's] own possession" (Titus 2:14),[5] which taps into this same rich seam of salvation history, except with Christ in the place of Yahweh (e.g., Ex. 19:5; Deut. 14:2; 26:18). Christ redeemed his people with his own life and purified them (1 John 1:7). They belong to him and are uniquely imprinted with his "messianic identity."[6] Their worth to him is demonstrated in the price he paid. And redeemed and cleansed, they are to be zealous for good works for his sake.

They have become heirs (*klēronomoi*, Titus 3:7) of eternal life as God's adopted children/sons (Rom. 8:14–17; Gal. 4:6–7). Gerald Bray explains: "What Christ the Son is by nature we have become by grace, and it is that standing, given to us by the indwelling presence of the Holy Spirit, that allows us to be 'heirs.'"[7] This is the fulfillment of God's Old Testament covenant promises of land and blessing (e.g., Gen. 22:17; 28:4; Lev. 20:24; Gal. 3:29).[8] As heirs, God's children have privilege, belonging, and certain rights to a future inheritance.

They are *not* who or what they *once* were (Titus 2:12; 3:3; cf. 1:12; 2:5, 8, 10). They *were* ignorant of God, disobedient to him, and duped by false guides,[9] enslaved to evil desires, and full of hate. Not anymore.

---

3   William D. Mounce, *Pastoral Epistles*, WBC 46 (Nashville: Thomas Nelson, 2000), 379.

4   Philip H. Towner, *The Letters to Timothy and Titus*, NICNT (Grand Rapids, MI: Eerdmans, 2006), 793–94; Abraham Kuruvilla, *1 & 2 Timothy, Titus: A Theological Commentary for Preachers* (Eugene, OR: Cascade, 2021), 224–25.

5   Andreas J. Köstenberger, *Commentary on 1–2 Timothy and Titus*, BTCP (Nashville: Holman Reference, 2017), 341.

6   Towner, *Letters*, 763.

7   Gerald L. Bray, *The Pastoral Epistles*, ITC (London: T&T Clark, 2019), 555.

8   Robert W. Yarbrough, *The Letters to Timothy and Titus*, PNTC (Grand Rapids, MI: Eerdmans, 2018), 550; Towner, *Letters*, 788.

9   J. N. D. Kelly, *The Pastoral Epistles: I & II Timothy, Titus* (London: Black, 1963), 250.

The decisive *spiritual* change they have undergone—having been saved by God; reborn, cleansed, and renewed by the Holy Spirit; justified and made heirs of eternal life (3:5–8)—has produced changed *hearts and lives* (e.g., 2:14; 3:8, 14–15; cf. 1:16). John Calvin rightly notes that this should keep believers humble and "prompt them to think that those who are outside the Church today may tomorrow be engrafted into it."[10]

On that note, while we might be struck by the ethnic stereotyping of all Cretans in such negative terms (1:12)—even when endorsed by one of their own—what should strike us more is that Christ gave himself for people like *this*, and that God saved them and poured out his Holy Spirit on them. Salvation is all of grace, and God's grace knows no bounds! *No one* is beyond redemption. Whatever they once were, these Cretans are now God's elect and Christ's own special people!

In short, believers' new identity is entirely initiated and effected by God in his triunity. It is God's work, not ours, and arises from our new relationship with him. It is exclusive to those who are saved and inclusive of Jew and Gentile. It has individual and corporate dimensions. And it has (pretemporal and recent) past, present, and future dimensions.

There are two further aspects to consider. First, they are the household of God (1 Tim. 3:15; cf. 1:4; 3:5). This is most apparent in that an elder/overseer[11] is "God's steward" (*oikonomos*, Titus 1:7—a term taken from estate or household management)—who will manage and care for God's household and be faithful to him as owner.[12] This theme also features in God's fatherhood (1:4), the training (*paideuousa*) of his grace (2:12),[13] our rebirth and status as heirs, the spiritual familial bonds (e.g., 1:4), Paul as God's "slave" (*doulos*, 1:1, 3), the nature of his and Titus's oversight,[14] the spiritual mothering of younger women

---

10 John Calvin, *The Second Epistle of Paul the Apostle to the Corinthians and the Epistles to Timothy, Titus, and Philemon*, trans. T. A. Smail, ed. David W. Torrance and Thomas F. Torrance, Calvin's Commentaries 10 (Grand Rapids, MI: Eerdmans, 1976), 378.

11 Both terms refer to the same office. Köstenberger, *Timothy and Titus*, 313.

12 Kuruvilla, *Timothy, Titus*, 204.

13 See D. Fürst, "*Paideuō*," in *NIDNTT* 3:775–79.

14 See Alan F. Tomlinson, "Purpose and Stewardship Theme within the Pastoral Epistles," in *EWTG* 60–62, 80.

by older women (2:3–5), and the concern for right relationships and conduct within actual households (2:2–10; cf. 1:11).[15]

Second, believers are ambassadors of God's word. Some have special responsibilities in that mission: Paul, through whom God manifested his word (1:3); Titus (1:5; 2:1, 7–8, 15; 3:1); the elders/overseers (1:9; cf. 1:11); and the older women (2:3). But no one is exempted. They all are saved through God's gospel (1:1, 3; 3:8), and each is to learn and believe, promote and confirm God's word in his or her life, and so be a witness to it among the Gentiles.[16] All believers, including the least of them in the culture of that day, could actively adorn his word or bring it public shame (2:5, 8, 10; cf. 1:6).

A Transformed Life

This new spiritual identity finds expression in the present age through visibly changed lives. The problem with the false teachers is this: they profess to know God, but their deeds deny their profession and prove they don't know God at all (1:16).[17] They and all unbelievers (*apistos*) have minds and consciences that are defiled (1:15),[18] and lives to match (3:3).

But *authentic* saving faith and knowledge produce (ever-increasing) godliness (*eusebeia*) and good works (1:1). Real faith is demonstrated in changed lives. This is possible only because the saving grace of God has appeared in Christ, training us to deny ungodliness and worldly passions (2:11–12) so we might live in the present age as heirs of *eternal* life (1:2; 3:7; cf. John 10:10), with lives characterized by self-control (*sōphronōs*), righteousness (*dikaiōs*), and godliness (*eusebōs*).

This requires both positive and negative instruction. God's grace trains us to stop doing certain things and start doing others. Likewise, Titus is to teach *and* rebuke and discipline (Titus 2:1, 15; 3:1–2, 8–9). Church leaders are to hold firmly to the message as

---

15 Köstenberger, *Timothy and Titus*, 456.
16 Philip H. Towner, "Pastoral Epistles," in *NDBT* 333.
17 Van Neste, "Our People," 196.
18 Marshall, *Pastoral Epistles*, 209.

it is taught everywhere and preach it faithfully, and rebuke and silence those who contradict it (1:9, 11). Older women are to bring younger women to their senses (*sōphronizō*)[19] and teach them what is good (2:4–5).

There are just two ways to live (e.g., Ps. 1),[20] and the only similarity between those two ways is the inexorable correspondence between a person's relationship with God and his or her lifestyle. As Jesus said, you will know them by their fruit (Matt. 7:16); and the fruit of sound faith is Christ-pleasing good works (Titus 2:7, 14; 3:1, 8, 14).[21] So believers must turn from one way of life and live out the other.

For example, instead of being morally repellent—ungodly (*asebeia*, 2:12), evil, defiled, detestable, warped, sinful, and self-condemned (1:12, 15–16; 2:8; 3:3, 11)—they are to be godly (1:1; 2:12) and pure (1:15; cf. 2:14). Elders/overseers, in particular, are to be above reproach, upright, and holy (1:6–8), and women/wives of all ages are to be reverent and pure (2:3–5). The opponents have their rules and rituals (1:11, 15), but inner cleansing comes only from God (2:14; 3:5).

Instead of being enslaved to passions and pleasures—including alcohol, money, food, and sexual indulgence (1:6–7, 11–12; 2:3, 6; 3:3)[22]—believers are to exercise self-control (*sōphrōn* and related words, 1:8; 2:2, 5–6, 12), showing moderation and good judgment, and being clear minded.[23] Leaders are to be faithful husbands and diligent fathers (1:6).[24] Older men are to be dignified and steadfast (2:2); and wives are to fulfill their duties at home (2:4–5). Slaves were to show all good faith (2:9–10).

---

19 Bruce W. Winter, *Roman Wives, Roman Widows: The Appearance of the New Women and the Pauline Communities* (Grand Rapids, MI: Eerdmans, 2003), 155–59.

20 Ben Witherington III, *A Socio-Rhetorical Commentary on Titus, 1–2 Timothy and 1–3 John*, vol. 1 of *Letters and Homilies for Hellenized Christians* (Downers Grove, IL: InterVarsity, 2006), ProQuest Ebook Central, https://ebookcentral.proquest.com/lib/moore/detail .action?docID=2030868), 96.

21 See Marshall, *Pastoral Epistles*, 227–31.

22 Winter, *Roman Wives*, 163–65.

23 Towner, *Letters*, 730. See Sean Christensen, "The Pursuit of Self-Control: Titus 2:1–14 and Accommodation to Christ," *JSPL* 6 (2016): 161–80.

24 Köstenberger, *Timothy and Titus*, 314.

Instead of being insubordinate (1:6, 10) and disobedient (1:16; 3:3), believers are to show due obedience and submission. Paul obeys his master, God (1:1, 3). Titus is to obey Paul's instructions. The churches are to accept the leaders Titus appoints and submit to his and their instruction (1:5, 9; 2:15; 3:10; cf. 1 Cor. 16:16). Church leaders are God's stewards, who answer to him (Titus 1:7). Children are to submit to their parents/fathers (1:6; cf. Eph. 6:1; Col. 3:20); wives, to their husbands (Titus 2:5; cf. Eph. 5:21–24; Col. 3:18; 1 Pet. 3:1–7); slaves, to their masters (Titus 2:9; cf. Eph. 6:5–8; Col. 3:22–24);[25] and all believers are willingly to submit to civic authorities, which, perhaps counterintuitively, is a good work for those who belong to Christ (Titus 3:1; cf. Rom. 13:1, 5; 1 Peter 2:13).[26] Paul does not address here the reciprocal duties of the other party or (where relevant) the theological grounds for these ordered relationships as he does elsewhere (e.g., Eph. 5:21–24; 6:1; 1 Tim. 2:11–14). The focus is polemical. The opponents' teaching and conduct destroys human households and God's household (Titus 1:11, 16). Sound teaching produces godly ordered social cohesion. Whatever their status, *every* believer can honor God through appropriate obedience and submission.

Instead of malice, envy, violence, and hate (1:7; 3:3), they are to love fellow believers and provide for any in need; they are to be gentle and courteous (2:2; 3:2, 14–15) and concerned for the salvation of all people (2:5, 8, 10). The opponents are motivated by greedy self-interest (1:11). But faithful church leaders are to be humble, not avaricious, to show hospitality and love the good (1:8–9). Older men are to be sound in their love (2:2). Wives are to be kind and to love their husbands and love their children (2:4). In short, believers are to imitate the generous, patient, self-giving love and grace of God in Christ (2:11, 14; 3:4, 6).

25 See the discussion of slavery in chap. 4, "The Household of God."
26 This doesn't rule out civil disobedience when the state requires what God forbids, or rule out seeking safety from violence or abuse or threats of violence within the family or church. On domestic abuse, see Claire Smith, "The Ultimate Distortion," chap. 8 in *God's Good Design: What the Bible Really Says about Men and Women*, 2nd rev. ed. (Kingsford, NSW: Matthias Media, 2019).

And instead of lies and deception, false professions of faith, slander, quarreling, discord, and divisions (1:12, 16; 2:3, 9; 3:2, 10), their speech is to be like God's speech. God does not lie; his word *is* truth, unchanging, trustworthy, sound/healthy, and life bringing (1:1–3, 9, 14; 3:8). Thus, Paul's words are meant to promote faith and knowledge of the truth (1:1). Titus's teaching is to be characterized by integrity, dignity, and sound/healthy speech (2:7–8). Church leaders' words of instruction and rebuke must be faithful to God's word, not hot-tempered or distracted by senseless, divisive arguments (1:9; 3:9). Older women's words (and lives) are to teach what is good (2:3–5). Believers are to bring honor, not shame, to God's word (2:5, 10) and speak evil of no one (3:2). By contrast, the opponents are babblers and deceivers who contradict sound teaching and destroy faith and households (1:10–14). *They* must be silenced!

The character and conduct of *every* believer matters—regardless of age, sex, or station in life, because Christ gave himself to redeem them all from all disobedience (2:14). Genuine faith always leads to changed lives. This is Paul's expectation of his apostolic ministry and of the teaching and godly examples of Titus, church leaders, and the older women (1:1, 5, 9; 2:1, 3–5, 15). This same nexus of faith and life is demonstrated *in the negative* with the opponents (1:16).

Finally, while many of the virtues and vices listed in Titus also appear in Hellenistic Jewish and Greco-Roman ethical teaching, their meaning here is not the same.[27] Not only does Paul expect believers to be very different from the surrounding culture and not to fit in with it; more significantly, the source, motivation, nature, goal, and means of acquiring these virtues are distinctly theological and Christological. The godly life is enabled by the Holy Spirit, poured out by God through Christ Jesus (3:5–6), and the fitting response to, and imitation of, the grace and goodness and loving-kindness of God in Christ (2:11; 3:4). It is the godliness that comes from faith in Christ and knowledge of

---

27 See Christensen, "Pursuit," 174–78; Köstenberger, *Timothy and Titus*, 484–87; Yarbrough, *Letters*, 500.

God's truth (1:1; 3:8). It follows, then, that the virtues Paul names are not simply suited to Cretan culture in such a way that would allow for different ethical ideals in other cultures.[28] They belong to a new way of *being* that will be fully realized only in the age to come. For now, we anticipate that eschatological existence in self-controlled, upright, and godly lives, while we await Christ's final appearing (2:12–13).

This does not come from us. It is possible only through—and exemplified by—the loving, gracious, saving, and educative intervention of God, in and through Jesus Christ and the Holy Spirit, in human history and his people's lives.[29] Believers *can* and *are* to live like this, solely because of who God is and what he has done and is doing.

———

All those whom God has saved are his own special people, chosen and loved by him. Our new identity and new existence are the work of the triune God, in fulfillment of his eternal salvation plan and, like God's mission itself, are orientated toward the future appearing of Christ. His people will (increasingly) have character and lives that align with his perfect character, purposes, and deeds. Despite what we once were, believers now produce fruit in keeping with repentance, are zealous for good works, and individually and corporately promote God's gospel mission.

But they will not and cannot do this on their own. God's grace in Christ will train them. Jesus Christ will purify them and, through the regenerating work of the Holy Spirit, enable their new lives. God's word has revealed his eternal promise. As God's servant and Christ's apostle, Paul proclaims it. He has left Titus on Crete to teach it and correct error, and to appoint church leaders, God's stewards, who will continue to proclaim and teach God's word, defend it from distortions, correct errors of doctrine and life, and model godly living, so that the witness and proclamation of God's saving gospel advances unhindered.

28 Knight, *Pastoral Epistles*, 316–18.
29 Towner, *Letters*, 749–50.

Epilogue

THE LETTERS TO TIMOTHY AND TITUS were written by Paul to trusted coworkers toward the end of his apostolic ministry. God's word was under attack in Ephesus and Crete, and the future of God's salvation project was (humanly speaking) at risk. The tasks of teaching God's truth and establishing God's people in the faith, and of silencing those who opposed both, were urgent. Given these similarities in the occasion of the letters, it is not surprising to find common features in all three—all the more so when two of them were written to the same person. The letters form a subgroup in the Pauline corpus.

The letters have a consistent focus on God's eternal plan to save a people for himself from all people, both Jews and Gentiles. His pre-temporal plan of salvation has been revealed and accomplished in history through the first appearing of Christ Jesus—in his incarnate life, ministry, atoning death, resurrection, and ascension—and will be completed when Christ appears again at the end of this age. At that time, God's plan will be fully realized, and God's people will receive eternal life. Until then, in the "now" between Christ's appearings, God's salvation is attained through faith in Christ Jesus and advances through the proclamation of the apostolic gospel. Paul's apostolic ministry is itself part of God's plan to reach the nations with the saving gospel.

These eschatological last days are also a time of apostasy and op-position to God's plan, God's word, and God's people. This spiritual opposition is manifested in false teachers, whose message and lives contradict apostolic teaching. These opponents must be stopped, and

God's saving word, preserved and advanced. Each letter identifies sound church leadership as a key means of ensuring this end. In the first instance, Paul's delegates, Timothy and Titus, are in the front line. They are to teach the truth and model godly living, ensure that churches are led by suitably gifted and godly men who will likewise teach and defend God's sound and healthy word, and rebuke and discipline those in the church who teach error and promote ungodliness.

But they will not be alone. All God's people, from the least to the greatest (in the culture of that day), are to learn, believe, be devoted to, adorn, and advance God's truth, and pursue godliness and be zealous for good works. Individually and corporately, they are to be observably different from unbelievers and to seek to further God's saving agenda in their engagement with wider society. Their hope is the future appearing of Jesus Christ in glory. In all this, they will be transformed and empowered by the Holy Spirit to live faithfully as God's elect; and, as God's household, they will be served and preserved through the sound teaching and pastoral ministry of godly church leaders.

While the letters have elements that speak to their first-century cultural setting, Paul's eyes are on the future of God's salvation plan, the nature and circumstances of which will not change in this present era. There was then and there is now only one God who saves, and only one mediator between God and all people, the God-man Jesus Christ, our great God and Savior, who came into the world and gave himself to save sinners, and who is now risen from the dead, vindicated and triumphant. He will appear again, when he will judge all the living and the dead. On that day, may we be among those "who have loved his appearing" (2 Tim. 4:8).

Recommended Resources

Books

Allen, David. *According to the Scriptures: The Death of Christ in the Old Testament and the New.* London: SCM, 2018.

Beale, G. K., and Benjamin L. Gladd. *Hidden but Now Revealed: A Biblical Theology of Mystery.* Downers Grove, IL: InterVarsity Press, 2014.

Beale, Gregory K. *A New Testament Biblical Theology: The Unfolding of the Old Testament in the New.* Grand Rapids, MI: Baker Academic, 2011.

Bray, Gerald L. *The Pastoral Epistles.* International Theological Commentary. London: T&T Clark, 2019.

Calvin, John. *The Second Epistle of Paul the Apostle to the Corinthians and the Epistles to Timothy, Titus, and Philemon.* Translated by T. A. Smail. Edited by David W. Torrance and Thomas F. Torrance. Calvin's Commentaries 10. Grand Rapids, MI: Eerdmans, 1976.

Fee, Gordon D. *1 and 2 Timothy, Titus.* New International Biblical Commentary. Peabody, MA: Hendrickson, 1988.

Fee, Gordon D. *God's Empowering Presence: The Holy Spirit in the Letters of Paul.* Peabody, MA: Hendrickson, 1994.

Fee, Gordon D. *Pauline Christology: An Exegetical-Theological Study.* Peabody, MA: Hendrickson, 2007.

Guthrie, Donald. *The Pastoral Epistles.* Tyndale New Testament Commentaries. 1957. Reprint, Leicester: Inter-Varsity Press, 1984.

Harris, Murray J. *Jesus as God: The New Testament Use of* Theos *in Reference to Jesus.* Grand Rapids, MI: Baker, 1992.

Harris, Murray J. *Prepositions and Theology in the Greek New Testament: An Essential Reference Resource for Exegesis.* Grand Rapids, MI: Zondervan. 2012.

Hughes, R. Kent, and Bryan Chapell. *1–2 Timothy and Titus (ESV Edition): To Guard the Deposit.* Wheaton, IL: Crossway, 2012.

Jeon, Paul S. *1 Timothy: A Charge to God's Missional Household.* Vol. 1. Eugene, OR: Pickwick, 2017.

Johnson, Luke Timothy. *The First and Second Letters to Timothy.* Anchor Bible 35A. New York: Doubleday, 2001.

Johnson, Luke Timothy. *Letters to Paul's Delegates: 1 Timothy, 2 Timothy, Titus.* The New Testament in Context. Valley Forge, PA: Trinity, 1996.

Kelly, J. N. D. *The Pastoral Epistles: I & II Timothy, Titus.* Black's New Testament Commentaries. London: Black, 1963.

Knight, George W. *Commentary on the Pastoral Epistles.* New International Greek Testament Commentary. Grand Rapids, MI: Eerdmans, 1992.

Köstenberger, Andreas J. *Commentary on 1–2 Timothy and Titus.* Biblical Theology for Christian Proclamation. Nashville. Holman Reference, 2017.

Kuruvilla, Abraham. *1 & 2 Timothy, Titus: A Theological Commentary for Preachers.* Eugene, OR: Cascade, 2021.

Lau, Andrew Y. *Manifest in the Flesh: The Epiphany Christology of the Pastoral Epistles.* Wissenschaftliche Untersuchungen zum Neuen Testament 2.86. Tübingen: Mohr Siebeck, 1996.

Marshall, I. Howard. *The Pastoral Epistles.* In collaboration with P. H. Towner. International Critical Commentary. Edinburgh: T&T Clark, 1999.

Mathews, Kenneth. *Genesis 1–11:26: An Exegetical and Theological Exposition of Holy Scripture.* New American Commentary. Nashville: B&H, 1996.

Morris, Leon. *The Apostolic Preaching of the Cross.* Grand Rapids, MI: Eerdmans, 1965.

Mounce, William D. *Pastoral Epistles.* Word Biblical Commentary 46. Nashville: Thomas Nelson, 2000.

Smith, Claire. *God's Good Design: What the Bible Really Says about Men and Women.* 2nd rev. ed. Kingsford, NSW: Matthias Media, 2019.

Stott, John. *The Message of 1 Timothy and Titus.* The Bible Speaks Today. London: Inter-Varsity Press, 1996.

Thornton, Dillon T. *Hostility in the House of God: An Investigation of the Opponents in 1 and 2 Timothy.* Bulletin for Biblical Research Supplements 15. Winona Lake, IN: Eisenbrauns, 2016.

Towner, Philip H. *The Goal of Our Instruction: The Structure of Theology and Ethics in the Pastoral Epistles.* Journal for the Study of the New Testament Supplement Series 34. Sheffield: JSOT, 1989.

Towner, Philip H. *The Letters to Timothy and Titus.* New International Commentary on the New Testament. Grand Rapids, MI: Eerdmans, 2006.

Wallace, Daniel B. *Greek Grammar beyond the Basics: An Exegetical Syntax of the New Testament.* Grand Rapids, MI: Zondervan, 1996.

Wieland, George M. *The Significance of Salvation: A Study of Salvation Language in the Pastoral Epistles.* Paternoster Biblical Monographs. Milton Keynes, UK: Paternoster, 2006.

Winter, Bruce W. *Roman Wives, Roman Widows: The Appearance of the New Women and the Pauline Communities.* Grand Rapids, MI: Eerdmans, 2003.

Witherington III, Ben. *A Socio-Rhetorical Commentary on Titus, 1–2 Timothy and 1–3 John.* Vol. 1 of *Letters and Homilies for Hellenized Christians.* Downers Grove, IL: IVP Academic, 2006. ProQuest Ebook Central, https://ebookcentral.proquest.com/lib/moore/detail.action?docID= 2030868.

Yarbrough, Robert W. *The Letters to Timothy and Titus.* The Pillar New Testament Commentary. Grand Rapids, MI: Eerdmans, 2018.

Articles

Akin, Daniel L. "The Mystery of Godliness Is Great: Christology in the Pastoral Epistles." In *Entrusted with the Gospel: Paul's Theology in the Pastoral Epistles,* edited by Andreas J. Köstenberger and Terry L. Wilder, 137–52. Nashville: B&H Academic, 2010.

Barcley, William B. "1 Timothy." In *Biblical Theological Introduction to the New Testament: The Gospel Realized,* edited by Michael J. Kruger, 357–75. Wheaton, IL: Crossway, 2016.

Barcley, William B. "2 Timothy." In *Biblical Theological Introduction to the New Testament: The Gospel Realized*, edited by Michael J. Kruger, 377–91. Wheaton, IL: Crossway, 2016.

Baugh, S. M. "A Foreign World: Ephesus in the First Century." In *Women in the Church: An Interpretation and Application of 1 Timothy 2:9–15*. 3rd ed., edited by Andreas J. Köstenberger and Thomas R. Schreiner, 25–64. Wheaton, IL: Crossway, 2016.

Baugh, S. M. " 'Savior of All People': 1 Tim. 4:10 in Context." *Westminster Theological Journal* 54 (1992): 331–40.

Bird, Michael F. "Sinner, Sin." In *Dictionary of Jesus and the Gospels*, edited by Joel B. Green, Scot McKnight, I. Howard Marshall, 1942–53. Downers Grove, IL: InterVarsity Press, 2013. ProQuest Ebook Central, https://ebookcentral.proquest.com/lib/moore/detail.action?docID=3316699.

Bumgardner, Charles J. "Kinship, Christian Kinship, and the Letters to Timothy and Titus." *Southeastern Theological Review* 7, no. 2 (2016): 3–17.

Christensen, Sean. "The Pursuit of Self-Control: Titus 2:1–14 and Accommodation to Christ." *Journal for the Study of Paul and His Letters* 6 (2016): 161–80.

Couser, Greg A. "The Sovereign Savior of 1 and 2 Timothy and Titus." In *Entrusted with the Gospel: Paul's Theology in the Pastoral Epistles*, edited by Andreas J. Köstenberger and Terry L. Wilder, 105–36. Nashville: B&H Academic, 2010.

Faber, Riemer A. " 'Evil Beasts, Lazy Gluttons': A Neglected Theme in the Epistle to Titus." *Westminster Theological Journal* 67 (2005): 135–45.

Fürst, D. "*Paideuō*." In *New International Dictionary of New Testament Theology*, edited by Colin Brown, vol. 3:775–81. Grand Rapids, MI: Zondervan, 1975–78.

Genade, Alfred A. "Life in the Pauline Letters (3): Life in the Pastoral Epistles." In *Biblical Theology of Life in the New Testament*, edited by F. P. Viljoen and A. J. Coetsee, 109–27. Cape Town: AOSIS, 2021.

Hafemann, Scott J. "Suffering." In *Dictionary of Paul and His Letters*, edited by Gerald F. Hawthorne, Ralph P. Martin, and Daniel G. Reid, 919–21. Downers Grove, IL: InterVarsity Press, 1993.

Haykin, Michael A. G. "The Fading Vision? The Spirit and Freedom in the Pastoral Epistles." *Evangelical Quarterly* 57 (1985): 291–305.

Ho, Chiao E. "Mission in the Pastoral Epistles." In *Entrusted with the Gospel: Paul's Theology in the Pastoral Epistles*, edited by Andreas J. Köstenberger and Terry L. Wilder, 241–67. Nashville: B&H Academic, 2010.

Johnson, Luke Timothy. "The Pedagogy of Grace: The Experiential Basis of Morality in Titus." In *"Ready for Every Good Work" (Titus 3:1): Implicit Ethics in the Letter to Titus*, edited by Ruben Zimmermann and Dogara Ishaya Manomi, 38–51. Contexts and Norms of New Testament Ethics 13. Wissenschaftliche Untersuchungen zum Neuen Testament 484. Tübingen: Mohr Siebeck, 2022.

Kidd, Reggie M. "Titus as *Apologia*: Grace for Liars, Beasts, and Bellies." *Horizons in Biblical Theology* 21 (1999): 185–209.

Köstenberger, Andreas J. "Ascertaining Women's God-Ordained Roles: An Interpretation of 1 Timothy 2:15." *Bulletin for Biblical Research* 7 (1997): 107–44.

Köstenberger, Andreas J. "Hermeneutical and Exegetical Challenges in Interpreting the Pastoral Epistles." In *Entrusted with the Gospel: Paul's Theology in the Pastoral Epistles*, edited by Andreas J. Köstenberger and Terry L. Wilder, 1–27. Nashville: B&H Academic, 2010.

Kruger, Michael J. "First Timothy 5:18 and Early Canon Consciousness: Reconsidering a Problematic Text." In *The Language and Literature of the New Testament: Essays in Honor of Stanley E. Porter's 60th Birthday*, edited by Lois Fuller Dow, Craig Evans, and Andrew Pitt, 680–700. Leiden: Brill, 2017.

Marshall, I. Howard. "The Christology of the Pastoral Epistles." *Studien zum Neuen Testament und seiner Umwelt* A, 13 (1988): 157–77.

Merkle, Benjamin L. "Ecclesiology in the Pastoral Epistles." In *Entrusted with the Gospel: Paul's Theology in the Pastoral Epistles*, edited by Andreas J. Köstenberger and Terry L. Wilder, 173–98. Nashville: B&H Academic, 2010.

O'Brien, Peter T. "Church." In *Dictionary of Paul and His Letters*, edited by Gerald F. Hawthorne, Ralph P. Martin, and Daniel G. Reid, 123–31. Downers Grove, IL: InterVarsity Press, 1993.

Pao, David W. "Let No One Despise Your Youth: Church and the World in the Pastoral Epistles." *Journal of the Evangelical Theological Society* 57 (2014): 743–55.

Porter, Stanley E. "The Pastoral Epistles: Common Themes, Individual Compositions. Concluding Reflections." *Journal for the Study of Paul and His Letters* 9 (2019): 167–82.

Rupprecht, Arthur A. "Slave, Slavery." In *Dictionary of Paul and His Letters*, edited by Gerald F. Hawthorne, Ralph P. Martin, and Daniel G. Reid, 881–83. Downers Grove, IL: InterVarsity Press, 1993.

Schnabel, Eckhard J. "Paul, Timothy, and Titus: The Assumption of a Pseudonymous Author and of Pseudonymous Recipients in the Light of Literary, Theological, and Historical Evidence." In *Do Historical Matters Matter to Faith? A Critical Appraisal of Modern and Postmodern Approaches to Scripture*, edited by James K. Hoffmeier and Dennis R. Magary, 383–403. Wheaton, IL: Crossway, 2012.

Schreiner, Thomas R. "An Interpretation of 1 Timothy 2:9–15: A Dialogue with Scholarship." In *Women in the Church: An Interpretation and Application of 1 Timothy 2:9–15*. 3rd ed., edited by Andreas J. Köstenberger and Thomas R. Schreiner, 163–225. Wheaton, IL: Crossway, 2016.

Schreiner, Thomas R. "'Problematic Texts' for Definite Atonement in the Pastoral and General Epistles." In *From Heaven He Came and Sought Her: Definite Atonement in Historical, Biblical, Theological, and Pastoral Perspective*, edited by David Gibson and Jonathan Gibson, 375–97. Wheaton, IL: Crossway, 2013.

Smith, Claire S. "Ethics of Teaching and Learning in Christianity Today: Insights from the Book of Titus." In *"Ready for Every Good Work" (Titus 3:1): Implicit Ethics in the Letter to Titus*, edited by Ruben Zimmermann and Dogara Ishaya Manomi, 237–54. Contexts and Norms of New Testament Ethics 13. Wissenschaftliche Untersuchungen zum Neuen Testament 484. Tübingen: Mohr Siebeck, 2022.

Smith, Claire S. "'Preaching': Toward Lexical Clarity for Better Practice." In *Theology Is for Preaching: Biblical Foundations, Method, and Practice*, edited by Chase R. Kuhn and Paul Grimmond, 34–52. Bellingham, WA: Lexham, 2021.

Stiekes, Gregory J. "Paul's Family of God: What Familial Language in the Pastorals Can and Cannot Tell Us about the Church." *Southeastern Theological Review* 7, no. 2 (2016): 35–56.

Thornton, Dillon. "Sin Seizing an Opportunity through the Commandments." *Horizons in Biblical Theology* 36 (2014): 142–58.

Tomlinson, F. Alan. "The Purpose and Stewardship Theme within the Pastoral Epistles." In *Entrusted with the Gospel: Paul's Theology in the Pastoral Epistles*, edited by Andreas J. Köstenberger and Terry L. Wilder, 52–83. Nashville: B&H Academic, 2010.

Towner, Philip H. "Christology in the Letters to Timothy and Titus." In *Contours of Christology in the New Testament*, edited by Richard N. Longenecker, 219–44. Grand Rapids, MI: Eerdmans, 2005.

Towner, Philip H. "1–2 Timothy and Titus." In *Commentary on the New Testament Use of the Old Testament*, edited by G. K. Beale and D. A. Carson, 891–918. Grand Rapids, MI: Baker Academic, 2007.

Towner, Philip H. "The Pastoral Epistles." In *New Dictionary of Biblical Theology*, edited by T. D. Alexander and Brian Rosner, 330–36. Leicester: Inter-Varsity Press, 2000.

Towner, Philip H. "The Present Age in the Eschatology of the Pastoral Epistles." *New Testament Studies* 32 (1986): 427–48.

Van Nes, Jermo. "The Pastoral Epistles: Common Themes, Individual Compositions? An Introduction to the Quest for the Origin(s) of the Letters to Timothy and Titus." *Journal for the Study of Paul and His Letters* 9 (2019): 6–29.

Van Neste, Ray. "'Our People': Ethics and the Identity of the People of God in the Letter to Titus." In *"Ready for Every Good Work" (Titus 3:1): Implicit Ethics in the Letter to Titus*, edited by Ruben Zimmermann and Dogara Ishaya Manomi, 189–201. Contexts and Norms of New Testament Ethics 13. Wissenschaftliche Untersuchungen zum Neuen Testament 484. Tübingen: Mohr Siebeck, 2022.

Westerholm, Stephen. "The Law and the 'Just Man' (1 Tim. 1:3–11)." *Studia Theologica* 36 (1982): 79–95.

Wieland, George M. "The Function of Salvation in the Letters to Timothy and Titus." In *Entrusted with the Gospel: Paul's Theology in the Pastoral*

Epistles, edited by Andreas J. Köstenberger and Terry L. Wilder, 153–72. Nashville: B&H Academic, 2010.

Wieland, George M. "Re-Ordering the Household: Misalignment and Realignment to God's *oikonomia* in 1 Timothy." In *Sin and Its Remedy in Paul*, edited by Nijay Gupta and John K. Goodrich, 147–60. Contours of Pauline Theology. Eugene, OR: Cascade, 2020.

Wieland, George M. "Roman Crete and the Letter to Titus." *New Testament Studies* 55 (2009): 338–54.

Wilder, Terry L. "Pseudonymity, the New Testament, and the Pastoral Epistles." In *Entrusted with the Gospel: Paul's Theology in the Pastoral Epistles*, edited by Andreas J. Köstenberger and Terry L. Wilder, 28–51. Nashville: B&H Academic, 2010.

Wolfe, B. Paul. "The Sagacious Use of Scripture." In *Entrusted with the Gospel: Paul's Theology in the Pastoral Epistles*, edited by Andreas J. Köstenberger and Terry L. Wilder, 199–218. Nashville: B&H Academic, 2010.

General Index

social status, 113
soteriology, 17, 66, 76
"sound" teaching, 41
speech, 26, 63, 135
stewardship, 48
style, 2
submission, 134
substitutionary death, 21, 31, 123
suffering, 71, 73, 78, 81, 86, 90, 96,
    99–104
suffering servant, 32, 102

teaching, 39, 41, 53, 55, 91–92, 94
temple, 49, 50
thanksgivings, 110
theology, 2, 66
theopneustos, 94
Timothy
    and appointing of overseers, 54
    cultural origins of, 5, 74, 87, 93–94
    divine appointment of, 22, 33
    versus false teaching, 25, 47, 59
    ministry of, 56, 71, 73, 92
    suffering of, 73, 78, 81, 89, 90, 92,
        96, 99, 101
    teaching of, 44, 52, 90
Titus
    ministry in Crete, 6
    proclamation of, 112
Towner, Philip, 57, 79
transformation, 84, 124–25, 132–36
trials, 100
Trinity, 23, 80, 97, 126, 131

"trustworthy saying" formula, 40–41
truth, 38–39, 41, 44

unbelief, 36
unbelievers, 33, 138
union with Christ, 12, 78, 82
universalism, 34

vanity, 26
vice lists, 60
victory, 86, 101
virtue lists, 60
vocabulary, 2, 4

washing, 124–25
water baptism, 124
weakness, 73, 104
widows, 51–52, 56, 100
Wieland, George, 14, 114
witness, 90
women, 30–31, 43, 51–52, 54, 55, 133
word of God
    as apostolic, 89–93
    attacks against, 37
    life of, 97–98
    as trustworthy and true, 112
    as written, 42–44, 92–95
words, 40
world, 65, 67

Yahweh, 12, 14, 21, 31, 74, 75, 87, 122,
    123, 130
Yarbrough, Robert, 77, 110n5

Zeus, 112, 113, 115

Scripture Index

New Testament Theology

The Beginning of the Gospel

From the Manger to the Throne

The Mission of the Triune God

Ministry in the New Realm

Christ Crucified

United to Christ, Walking in the Spirit

Hidden with Christ in God

To Walk and to Please God

The Appearing of God Our Savior

Perfect Priest for Weary Pilgrims

The God Who Judges and Saves

The Joy of Hearing

Edited by Thomas R. Schreiner and Brian S. Rosner, this series presents clear, scholarly overviews of the main theological themes of each book of the New Testament, examining what they reveal about God and his relation to the world in the context of the overarching biblical narrative.

For more information, visit **crossway.org**.